Hans Alfred Müller

Sheep

Everything about Housing, Care,
Feeding, and Sicknesses
Special Chapter: Milking and What to Do with the Milk,
Shearing and Processing the Wool

With Color Photographs by Eminent Animal Photographers and Drawings
by Günther Marks

Translated from the German by Rita and Robert Kimber
Consulting Editor: Paula Simmons

BARRON'S

New York • London • Toronto • Sydney

Photos on covers:
Front cover: Merino sheep with lamb. Back cover: Above, left: Coburg fox sheep; Above, right: Bottle-feeding Skudden lambs; Below, left: Shearing a sheep in a pen; Below, right: Merino ewe with twin lambs in a lambing pen. Inside front cover: Milk sheep in the backyard; the hobbyist sheep farmer is motivated by enjoyment of the animals more than by economic necessity. Inside back cover: Two young Skudden lambs. Skudden sheep are very popular in Europe. This breed originated in eastern Prussia (Germany).

Photo credits:
Angermayer: Page 28, above, right, and below, right; Angermayer/Freudenberger: Page 27; Dittrich: Page 28, below, left; Eisl: Page 9, middle, left; König: page 9, middle, right; Lehmann: Back cover, below, right; Müller: Page 28, above, left; Reinhard: Page 9, above, left, and below, right; page 38, above and below; Page 48; inside back cover; back cover, above, left and right; Scherz: Page 9, below, left; Schulz: Page 47, above, left; Silvestris/Buchholz: Back cover, below, left; Skogstad: Front cover; inside front cover; Page 9, above, right; Page 37; Wothe: Page 10; Page 47, above, right, and below.

English translation © Copyright 1989 by Barron's Educational Series, Inc.

© Copyright 1984 by Gräfe and Unzer GmbH, Munich, West Germany
The title of the German book is *Shafe als Haustiere*.

All inquiries should be addressed to:
Barron's Educational Series, Inc.
250 Wireless Boulevard
Hauppauge, NY 11788

Library of Congress Catalog Card No. 88-33300
International Standard Book No. 0-8120-4091-0

Library of Congress Cataloging-in-Publication Data

Muller, Hans Alfred
Sheep, everything about, care, feeding, and sicknesses ...
Includes index.
1. Sheep. I. Title.
SF375.M8513 1989   636.3   88-33300
ISBN 0-8120-4091-0

Printed and bound in Hong Kong
9012   4900   987654321

About the author:
Hans Alfred Müller, D.V.M., was born in 1947. After studying veterinary medicine at the University of Giessen, he did research in various areas, including parasitology and the behavior of domestic animals. He has had his own veterinary practice for several years.

Dr. Müller is especially interested in livestock breeding and in animal husbandry. He has been raising sheep as well as goats and Haflingen horses on his farm for many years.

Important Note:
This book discusses the purchase, care, and breeding of sheep. Since even careful supervision and a good fence offer no absolute guarantee against the sheep breaking out of their pasture and possibly causing property damage or traffic accidents, liability insurance is highly recommended. Insurance companies have policies designed especially for owners of animals.

Electric fences that are hooked up to regular electric lines rather than being battery-operated may be installed only by licensed electricians.

Sheep owners who want to sell sheep milk or cheese and meat have to conform to regulations affecting the sale of foodstuffs. Since regulations vary from country to country and from state to state, sheep owners should consult official veterinarians in their localities or other local authorities for information on this subject before marketing sheep products.

39262 ◆ Ingram 8/94

Contents

Contents

Preface

Keeping sheep has been an activity of great importance to humans for thousands of years. Even today sheep form the basis of economic survival in many countries, just as they have in the past. They provide nutritious food in the form of milk and meat, as well as wool, a prized raw material for clothing. With the coming of the industrial age, the old ways of keeping sheep began to change, and in many parts of the world the methods of modern agriculture are now used in sheep raising with the result that new, highly efficient breeds now produce record amounts of wool and meat.

The majority of sheep are tended, as they always have been, by shepherds who wander through the countryside with their flocks from pasture to pasture. In recent years, however, sheep farming on a much smaller scale has gained in importance: Many families have started to keep two or three animals or a small flock on their own piece of land. For them, tending these ancient, useful domestic animals is a source of pleasure and relaxation and provides welcome relief from the hectic pace of modern life. Because of their modest demands, sheep are ideal for people who have never kept farm animals but would like to raise at least part of their food in a natural way. This book is meant to serve them as a reliable guide.

The first chapter tells you what sheep breeds are most suitable for your particular situation. The author, an experienced sheep keeper and veterinarian, discusses popular American and European breeds and answers all the questions that have to do with the daily business of having sheep. Among other things, you'll find out everything you need to know about housing and management of sheep, including the raising of lambs. In another chapter, signs of illness, the typical course that illnesses take in sheep, and treatments are discussed. You'll learn about first-aid measures that may enable you to treat some of your sheep's minor illnesses and injuries yourself.

A special chapter tells you how to use and process the various products of sheep. Here you'll find advice and instructions on how to milk sheep and what to do with the milk, how to shear sheep, and how to process and use the wool, and, finally, how to slaughter an animal and what to do with the various cuts of meat.

Color photographs by eminent animal photographers, published here for the first time, show interesting breeds of sheep, including shots of gamboling lambs that capture the animals' irresistible charm. Instructive drawings illustrate important details, showing, among other things, how to build movable fences, barns, and feeding racks. The author and the publisher wish to thank the photographers, who made their best pictures available for this book, as well as Günther Marks, who made the drawings. Last, but not least, they want to express thanks to Mrs. Ulrike Müller, Mrs. Ingeborg Müller-Sieslak, and a number of owners of milk sheep, whose extensive knowledge and experience has contributed greatly to the successful completion of the special chapter on processing sheep products.

Our Domestic Sheep

From Wild to Domestic Sheep

All breeds of domestic sheep are descended from wild European and Asian sheep, the most important of which are the mouflon (see color photo on page 28, above, right) and the argali. The domestication of sheep reaches far back in human history, probably more than 10,000 years.

Although domestic sheep have retained the basic characteristics of their wild ancestors over thousands of years, some major differences started to emerge as economic productivity became a more significant factor in sheep raising. Different local environments, selection by humans of individual animals for breeding purposes, and geographic isolation of some flocks all contributed to regional differences and culminated in distinct regional breeds.

Regional breeds are well adapted to the conditions of their geographic localities. They require only minimal care and make good use of the poorer forage plants that grow in their areas. Their productivity (meat and wool) is quite impressive given the traditional low-input methods of maintenance (grazing on open pastures) but falls short, of course, of the results achieved with selectively bred animals from specialized breeds and with better feeding and more intensive management.

This process of domestication and evolution into different breeds took place—almost imperceptibly—over long periods of time.

By contrast, the last few decades have seen radical changes in all industrialized countries in the way livestock is managed and bred. These changes, which have occurred with a speed that seems dizzying when viewed against the long history of human involvement in the domestication of animals, have resulted in a drastic reduction in numbers of breeds. This process has not affected sheep as dramatically as it has cattle, pigs, and poultry, but even here the trend toward fewer and more economically productive breeds has accelerated in recent years. Today a commercial sheep breeder's goal is to achieve top productivity under industrial conditions. The old-fashioned local strains that evolved as sheep adapted to their environment have been abandoned and have either been completely eliminated or continue to exist only in small numbers.

In the early stages of domestication and for a long time thereafter, sheep were kept exclusively for the meat. A mutation, that is, a variation in a hereditary characteristic, gave rise to a second economic use for sheep, namely their wool. *Wild* and *hair sheep* have a thick winter coat that consists of long, smooth guard hairs and an undercoat of fine, wooly hair. This entire coat is gradually shed in the spring and replaced by a shorter, smooth summer coat. By contrast, the coat of specialized *wool sheep* is made up entirely of wool hairs that keep growing, so that the animals must be sheared once a year.

In the Middle Ages the Spaniards bred some wool sheep from the Near East to obtain a superior fleece and created the merino breed, and from the eighteenth century on merino sheep have formed the basis of modern fine-wool breeds. In those earlier periods the main purpose of keeping sheep was the production of high-quality fine wool. By the nineteenth century, however, the Industrial Revolution ushered in changes that were further accelerated by the discovery of artificial fibers and by mass production of sheep wool in North and South America and in Australia. Worldwide, the number of domestic sheep today is estimated at over a billion.

The Characteristics of Sheep

Sheep belong to the mammalian order Artiodactyla and within that order to the even-toed ungulates. They are ruminants, and like cattle, antelopes, and goats, they have horns, live in herds, and feed on plants.

Like their wild ancestors, our domestic sheep are quite defenseless. They can respond to the

Our Domestic Sheep

threat of a predator only with flight or by seeking the protection the herd affords. Even rams with horns use them almost exclusively for ritual battles with rivals and hardly ever in self-defense against other kinds of animals. Only ewes occasionally defend their newborn lambs against a fox or a small dog. The senses of sheep, especially those of smell, hearing, and the ability to detect movement within the field of vision, were originally very acute but have declined somewhat in the course of domestication. One trait that has remained unchanged is the crowding together and taking off in panicked flight in response to anything that stimulates the slightest fear. The horny layer on the tips of their toes enables sheep to walk almost endlessly on hard ground and protects the toes when the animals jump and climb on rocks. On the soft ground of pastures or on thick bedding in the barn, however, these horny parts of the hooves are not worn down sufficiently and must be trimmed and corrected to prevent malformations and hoof diseases.

Like all horned ungulates, sheep have incisors only in the lower jaw. These incisors are pressed against a horny plate in the upper jaw to rip off grasses and other plants, and they also work well in peeling the bark from twigs and branches. This debarking can, however, cause serious damage to trees and shrubs, especially if the animals are hungry. In addition to the six incisors and two canines in the lower jaw, sheep also have twenty molars, five on each side in both the upper and lower jaws.

The Function of Chewing the Cud

Because it is a ruminant, a sheep has a large stomach that is made up of several parts or chambers and enables the animal to digest highly fibrous food (see drawing on this page). The *rumen*, which takes up much of the abdominal cavity, serves as a fermenting chamber. Here the only minimally chewed food is acted on by bacteria and minute protozoa, which break down the cellulose so that the protein is released from the plant cells and can be digested.

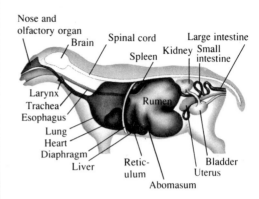

The internal organs of a sheep. The complex stomach with the huge rumen is impossible to overlook.

Sheep are able to eat a large amount of food in a relatively short time. During periods of rest, this food is chewed again in what is called rumination or chewing the cud. What happens is that portions of food are regurgitated from the rumen via the *reticulum* back into the mouth, where they are thoroughly masticated and then swallowed again. Only food that is chewed sufficiently fine can pass on to the *omasum*, then to the *abomasum*—which corresponds more or less to our stomach—and from there to the intestines.

The function of the rumen is to convert plant matter that is high in cellulose and would otherwise be nutritionally almost worthless into valuable and digestible nutrients. The conditions in the rumen must remain stable at a pH value (degree of acidity) between 6.2 and 7.0. Because of the complex nature of the activities in the rumen, sheep are particularly vulnerable to upsets caused by wrong diet. The wrong kind of food or food eaten too fast can quickly raise or lower the pH value in the rumen, as can a sudden shift from one kind of food to another. If too much gas forms, the rumen can become dangerously bloated. These conditions can endanger an animal's life if proper measures are not

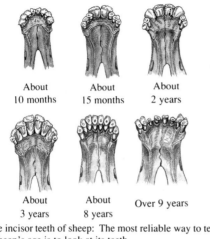

About 10 months	About 15 months	About 2 years

About 3 years	About 8 years	Over 9 years

The incisor teeth of sheep: The most reliable way to tell a sheep's age is to look at its teeth.

immediately taken. You should therefore try to prevent these conditions from developing by feeding your sheep a good, well-balanced diet

Determining a Sheep's Age

The best way to tell a sheep's age is to look at its front teeth (see drawing above). The molars are examined for this purpose only in dead animals because it is too hard to get a really good look at them in live sheep. The middle pair of incisors in a sheep's lower jaw are usually referred to as number 1. Incisors numbers 2 and 3 are the adjacent teeth on both sides, and the canines are the two outermost teeth.

By the time a lamb is four weeks old, all its temporary front teeth have formed. These milk teeth come in starting with the center teeth and are all fully developed by the time the lamb is six to nine months old, at which point they form an almost solid ridge. The change from milk teeth to permanent teeth also starts at the center, the first pair being replaced between months 15 and 18. The next two pairs of permanent incisors grow in at 20 to 25 months and at 27 to 35 months, respectively. The new canines develop when a sheep is three to three and a half years old. At this point all the temporary teeth have given way to permanent teeth This timetable may vary slightly in different breeds and between the sexes, and it may be affected by the kind of food the sheep eat, but on the whole you can assume that

• a sheep with one pair of permanent incisors is about a year and a half old
• it is two years old if it has two pairs of permanent incisors
• it is three years old if it has three pairs of permanent teeth and it is at least three and a half years old if its canines are permanent

The teeth wear down over the years and also assume a longer shape. Usually by the time a sheep is about nine years old, some of the teeth are worn down to mere stumps, and gaps develop between the teeth that remain. Old sheep therefore find it harder to eat and tend to become more and more emaciated.

Above: Spectacled sheep and German milk sheep
Center: White mountain sheep and Finn sheep
Below: Black-faced meat sheep and coarse-wooled regional sheep from Pomerania

Our Domestic Sheep

Sheep Facts and Figures

Body temperature	101 to 104°F (38.5–40°C)
Pulse rate per minute	70 to 80
Need for water of a sheep weighing 130 to 220 pounds (60–100 kg)	1 ½ quarts to 1 ½ gallons (1.5–7 liters)
Type of cycle	Polyestrous (repeatedly fertile about every 3 weeks) in the fall
Sexual maturity	Approximately 7 months
Ready for breeding	Approximately 8 months
Length of cycle	17 (14 to 30) days
Length of estrus	2 (1 to 3) days
Ovulation	Toward the end of estrus
Length of gestation	150 (145 to 155) days
Offspring per birth	1 to 2
Reproductive period	1 to 8 years
Readiness for slaughter	4 to 6 months for spring lamb, up to 2 years for regular lamb

Anatolian mountain sheep with newborn lamb. Shortly after giving birth the mother turns to her lamb and carefully licks it dry.

Sheep Breeds

Hair Sheep

In various parts of the world even today there are some hair sheep that don't need to be shorn. In Europe, for instance, there are a few small flocks of *Soay* sheep, a breed that was common all over England during the Middle Ages. The winter coat of these sheep is hardly any longer than that of the *mouflon* and can be plucked out in the spring. If this is not done, the coat is simply replaced by the shorter summer coat. Although sheep wool is a prized commodity and short in supply, the cost of having a few animals shorn can be higher than the price obtained for a small amount of unsorted raw wool. For this reason the hairy coat of some of these primitive sheep breeds may once more prove useful.

The small, usually reddish brown *Cameroon sheep* that originally came from Africa has gained increasing favor among people who keep sheep as a hobby.

Milk Sheep

The *German milk sheep* (see color photos on page 9 and on inside cover) is ideally suited as a family sheep. In fact, it seems not to fare as well in a large flock because it needs more individual care. Milk sheep do require a fairly large pasture on which the individual animals can be tethered, however. Because of their prolificacy and high milk production, German milk sheep have earned a special place among sheep breeds—although they are rare in the United States and Canada. Multiple births of two to four lambs are common. Anyone who has tasted the fresh milk of these animals will attest to its delicious flavor. Sheep's milk is less watery and contains more protein, fat, and vitamins than cow's milk. A glass of sheep's milk is nutritionally richer than a glass of cow's milk.

The German milk sheep originated in marshy areas of Germany and is today a breed of proven quality that is raised in many parts of the world. It is a large, white sheep with a narrow, unwooled face, long, thin ears, naked legs, and a thin, naked tail. A ewe produces 4½ to 11 pounds (2–5 kg) of milk per day, with a fat content of 6 to 7%. This adds up to between 880 and 1540 pounds (400–700 kg) a year. In addition, the animal produces 9 to 11 pounds (4–5 kg) of raw wool, which is between 4½ and 5½ pounds (2–2.5 kg) of pure wool. A fully grown ram weighs between 220 and 330 pounds (100–150 kg); the weight of a ewe is around 150 to 175 pounds (70–80 kg). The lambs grow quickly and mature early; ram lambs attain 110 to 130 pounds (50–60 kg) by the time they are six months old.

German milk sheep have proven particularly suitable for small operations with one to eight ewes. Their primary economic return is their milk, which can of course be used by the family but also commands a price well above that of cow's or goat's milk from people who like sheep's milk.

A second economic benefit of milk sheep is their meat production. Because milk sheep have so many lambs, some of them can be raised either for the family's table use or to be sold for slaughter. Economically, the wool is less important than the milk and meat, although it is quite plentiful and of reasonably good quality. If you have the time and enjoy spinning, knitting, and weaving, this is the best use for it.

Milk sheep come in heat only in the fall, which means that the lambs are born in the spring.

In addition to the white milk sheep there are also dark brown as well as mottled milk sheep, but they are not as productive as the white strain. The *French milk sheep*, however, is very productive. In France, various places in the United States, and in parts of England, large flocks are retained for the production of milk for Roquefort cheese. The *Friesian* breed is particularly renowned for its milking capacity and is now kept by many British breeders. It can yield up to 6½ pounds (3 kg) daily for two months, after its young have been weaned at about six weeks of age, and will continue to milk well into the autumn.

Sheep Breeds

Regional Breeds

A characteristic of regional breeds—breeds whose occurrence is restricted to limited geographic areas—is their hardiness and ability to thrive with only minimal care. These sheep are practically never sick, they can walk long distances, they are fertile and have a good mothering instinct, and they thrive even on poor food. However, the line between regional strains and breeds that have been deliberately developed for high economic yield is not always clear-cut. The *merino sheep*, for instance, was originally a regional breed but is now valued in many parts of the world for its economic potential in the production of both wool and meat.

Some highly specialized breeds and crosses of breeds having certain desired traits may outperform regional breeds, particularly in terms of meat production, and thus bring a higher economic return, but older regional breeds are periodically used for crossbreeding to add their good qualities to highly bred flocks. The *Rhön sheep* is a rather large animal with a black face and fine-boned, white legs. It is well adapted to the harsh conditions of higher altitudes. The *Coburg fox sheep* (see color photo on back cover, above, left) owes its name to the fox-red color of its face and legs and sports a "golden fleece." The lambs are reddish brown at birth. The *Bentheim sheep* is characterized by its arched "ram's nose." It also has black patches around the eyes. The *Kärnten spectacled sheep* (see color photo on page 9) looks very similar but is rarer. *Mountain sheep* (see color photos on pages 9 and 10) are more widespread because of their high fertility rate and their out-of-season breeding. They have a modest fleece of slightly wavy wool, an open face, and a distinct ram's nose. The ears are long and wide and droop down. Most mountain sheep are white, but there is also a brown strain. Sexual maturity sets in early, young ewes breeding at six to eight months. Their lambing percentage lies well above 200%, and because the ewes breed out of season, mountain lambs may be born any time of

year. These animals are strong and healthy, have tough hoofs, are excellent climbers, and have water-repellent coats, so that they thrive at high altitudes and in wet climates.

Special Meat Breeds

In contrast to the sheep we have discussed so far, which are found mainly in their regions of origin, merino and other breeds of meat sheep are geographically much more widespread. Their production of both meat and wool exceeds that of regional breeds, and they are therefore as a general rule better suited where economic profitability is the primary concern.

Merino sheep with lambs.

Merino (See color photo on front cover): Merino sheep are medium large and white and have a wedge-shaped head with a shock of wool on the forehead and good-sized, broad ears that point slightly downward. They are hardy, fertile, and fast growing and raise a large percentage of their lambs.

Merino sheep are not only good meat producers but are also kept for their excellent wool. They thrive both on open range and on fenced pastures. Because they breed out of season, they can lamb three times within two years. Mature lambs weigh up to 280 pounds (130 kg), ewes, 150 to 175 pounds (70–80 kg).

Merino meat sheep : This breed is considerably less common. It originated in Lower Saxony, Germany, where it still makes up about a quarter of the sheep population.This strain, too, breeds out of season and is especially suitable for raising milk-fed lambs.

Black-faced German meat sheep: (See color photo on page 8): This breed is similar both in appearance and production to *Suffolk sheep*, which originated in England. The breeders' goal with these breeds, as with all meat breeds, is to increase meat production and thus profitability. Of course meat production is not the only measure of profitability; hardiness, adaptability, fertility, and mortality must also be taken into account. Suffolk and black-faced German meat sheep perform well in all these areas. Suffolk sheep, which made a significant contribution to the development of the German black-facedbreed, are still occasionally crossed in even today.

The lambs are black at birth, and the smooth-haired face and the legs remain black while the fleece grows in white.

White-faced German meat sheep: This strain produces in the same range as its black-faced relative, but the maximum weight of mature animals lies somewhat higher, with up to 330 pounds (150 kg) for rams and 200 pounds (90 kg) for ewes. This breed has white legs and a white face with a pronounced shock of wool on the broad forehead.

Blue-faced German meat sheep: This strain, too, resembles the black-faced meat sheep in appearance and production. In this breed, however, the legs and the open face are covered with blue to bluish gray hair.

Texel sheep: This Dutch meat sheep, which is named after the island of Texel, is especially well adapted to fenced grazing. Texel sheep are early maturing, fertile, and hardy. The carcass is very meaty so that the dressed-out weight is high. Texel sheep breed in season. Because of their high meat productivity, Texel rams are often mated with milk sheep ewes. This improves the quality of the lambs destined for slaughter.

Line sheep: Line sheep were originally a German regional breed, but as a result of scientific breeding and crossbreeding, today's line sheep are more properly classified with the meat sheep since their meat production is comparable to that of other breeds of meat sheep. Early maturity, high fertility, adaptability, hardiness, and a high survival rate of the lambs characterize this breed.

Other productive meat breeds include the *brown faced meat sheep* and the *Charollais* sheep. Both are comparable to other meat breeds in uses and productivity.

Other Popular Breeds

Wool sheep, many of which are widely kept in the United States, Canada, and England, include: the *Cheviot*, a medium wool breed that was developed in Scotland; the *Corriedale*, a crossbred sheep from New Zealand; *Hampshire*, *Oxford Down*, *Shropshire*, *Southdown*, *Suffolk*, and *Dorset* sheep, all medium wool breeds of English origin; the fine wool *Rambouillet* from France; the *Colombia* and the *Targhee*, crossbred wool sheep developed in the United States; the long wool *Romney* and *Lincoln*, both from England; and the *Tunis*, which originated in North Africa and Asia.

Considerations Before You Buy

Economic Enterprise or Hobby?

A lot of people acquire a few sheep without any intention of embarking on sheep raising according to the rules of agricultural economics. For them the prime motive is often the pleasure of having a few animals of one's own or the desire to put to use a bit of land that is lying idle. Occasionally the decision to buy sheep is based on the desire to produce some of one's own food, like milk, cheese, and meat, and perhaps wool as well.

There is a difference between the agricultural enterprise of sheep raising on the one hand and keeping a few sheep as a hobby on the other. This difference can have significant legal consequences if, for example, you happen to live in an area where local zoning ordinances prohibit commercial farming. Be sure to investigate these regulations before you proceed any further with your plans.

Housing and Other Requirements

If you have studied extensively what sheep need to thrive, you have made a good beginning. The conditions for success are .

• a readiness on your part to invest time and effort in the conscientious care and maintenance of your animals
• sufficient space for housing the animals in a barn or other shelter and a place for storing feed
• a pasture that is large enough for the number of animals contemplated

You should have a realistic idea of the kind of pasture and the amount of feed and care sheep require if you want to avoid disappointment and hope to enjoy years of having your own healthy animals.

Anybody who is thinking of acquiring a larger number of sheep with the intention of breeding them or who might want to make a living as a sheep farmer must check very carefully if conditions are right for such an enterprise. If they are, the best way to prepare is to work with a shepherd for awhile to acquire the necessary knowledge and experience.

How Much Time and Money Are Involved?

If you have only a few sheep and keep them on a pasture during the summer, the time spent on them is minimal. This is assuming that they have access to drinking water and there is plenty of forage. In the winter, when the sheep are inside or on a pasture with an open shelter, the animals must be fed, which takes a little more time. Then there is the question of what to do when you are away from home. How long can you leave your sheep alone without anyone to look after them?

As long as they have enough food and water, sheep do fine for several days on their own. If there is a brook running through the pasture, no care may be needed for several weeks. Depending on the setup, someone should check anywhere from once a day to once every four days to make sure everything is all right.

Accidents, as when a sheep rolls over on its back and cannot get up again, may result in the death of the animal and can probably never be completely eliminated. Of course, the more closely a flock is supervised, the smaller the chance of mishaps. This is particularly important to remember when the ewes are pregnant and after the birth of the lambs.

Keeping sheep in a pasture involves some expenses, such as

• building and/or maintaining fencing and a shelter
• rent for land if it is leased
• fertilizer for the pasture and, in most cases, grain or other supplemental feed for the animals

If sheep are kept under an intensive management system, especially if you keep milking sheep, the daily time investment is considerably higher all year-round. Lambing time and special chores (hoof care, shearing, and cleaning out manure) always require some extra hours.

Can a Herding Animal Like a Sheep Be Kept Singly?

Keeping a single sheep runs counter to the animal's instinctive needs. If at all feasible, at least two sheep should be kept together. If for some compelling reason you can keep only one, you must either spend a lot of time with it yourself or give it another kind of animal for a companion. Milk sheep or orphan lambs that were bottle-fed and therefore have formed a real attachment to humans suffer the least if kept singly.

Rams, especially if they have been hand raised, can be a source of danger to children because of their tendency to chase and butt people. Castrated animals are less aggressive.

What to Watch for When Buying Sheep

If you are just setting out in the sheep business, I would suggest that you buy two ewes, if possible directly from a breeder. There you can observe the animals and get a good sense of their state of health. If for no other reason than to maintain his or her reputation, the breeder will try to sell you only healthy animals. Also, you can turn to him or her later if questions or problems arise. You have none of these benefits if you buy your animals at a livestock auction.

Here are a few pointers on how to assess a sheep's health:

• Healthy sheep take an active interest in their surroundings. Their eyes should be clear and bright.
• Their fleece is smooth and their overall shape

round. But don't buy lambs with pot bellies—often an indication of faulty diet and infrequent feeding.
• Their legs and hoofs are healthy.
• Wool around the tail and rump should not be smeared with manure; this indicates diarrhea.
• If the fleece is thick, you must use your hands to tell how well fed an animal is.
• If you have some reason to doubt the age that is given for the animal, check the condition of its teeth (see page 8).
• It is hard to say how much you should pay for sheep because the prices fluctuate so much. Animals bred for top performance may be very costly. The bids for prize-winning rams at ram auctions can be in the thousands of dollars. If you are interested in purebred sheep, you can ask for information at a local breeder's association.
• A lamb taken from the flock should be about three or four months old. At the other end of the scale, a ewe that is five or six years old is beyond its best years and is regarded as an old sheep.
• If you plan to raise registered sheep, you should from the very beginning buy animals with registration papers. If you don't have any special breeding ambitions, there is no need to spend money on expensive, registered purebreds. Sheep are vaccinated against certain diseases only if special circumstances require it; they are not expected to have vaccination records provided for cats and dogs.
• In today's world it may be advisable for any animal owner to consider liability insurance. The greatest risk is that an animal might cause a car accident. There are also policies that insure the owner of animals against loss resulting from illness, death, and theft, but given the high cost of the premiums, you may decide you are better off taking the risk yourself.

Making the Right Choice

When you decide what breed of sheep to select, you should be very clear about your own situation and expectations. Are you interested in a low-cost, low-input enterprise or in intensive management? The difference between the two systems is how much time and money you invest for pasture management (fertilization, setting up a system for rotational grazing, and so on), grain and other feed supplements, medication, and buildings. An extreme example of low-input sheep farming is to let a small flock of hardy sheep graze year-round on a remote piece of land without feeding them grain and without additional fertilization of the pasture. A rigorous system of intensive production, on the other hand, may mean rotating sheep on regularly fertilized pastures or keeping them in a barn and giving them large grain rations. The line between the two systems is fluid. The old-fashioned regional breeds are better adapted to the low-input system;

the specialized meat and wool breeds, especially milk sheep, are most productive under an intensive system.

The profitability of sheep farming depends largely on the fertility of the ewes (number of lambs per year) and the weight gain of the lambs. Good meat sheep that are intensively managed can average a prolificacy rate of 200%, which means that two lambs per ewe are raised annually. By contrast, older breeds usually produce only one lamb per year even under good conditions. The older breeds also produce less meat per animal. If you are primarily interested in economic return, you would therefore select one of these older breeds only because one of their traits, like hardiness in adverse climate, minimal need for care, or the ability to make efficient use of poor pasture, is important to you.

Care and Maintenance

Different Methods of Sheep Farming

Herding sheep on an open range has been the traditional method of keeping sheep since time immemorial, and even today many sheep still live that way in the mountainous regions of the West. The image of a shepherd and flock, accompanied by herding dogs, is familiar to us all. However, the more usual modern practice is to graze sheep on fenced pastures to which the flocks are taken by truck. Western ranches are quite large—often with as many as 10,000 acres of land and 1,000 to 2,000 sheep.

Taking care of a flock of 100 to 300 ewes is a full-time job for a farmer who is trying to make a living from his or her animals. Plenty of land for grazing and a large shelter that can accommodate the flock during extremely cold weather or when there is heavy snow are needed. The barn or shelter is also used to store hay for winter. Growing enough feed, looking after the animals' health, supervising the lambing, and raising the lambs require not only specialized knowledge on the part of the shepherd but also a lot of hard work. Seeing a shepherd working together smoothly with his dogs is an impressive sight and the result of skills that are acquired only through long-term, daily work with the animals.

Keeping sheep on fenced pastures is gradually replacing the traditional method of flocks roaming the countryside with their shepherds. Fenced flocks are usually smaller. Whether you can keep a few sheep this way depends on the kind of soil that is available, on the density of population, and on the local pattern of agriculture. In many areas housing developments, industry, and roads have reduced the land that was at one time available for farming, and if open spaces remain that are large enough for farming, they are often taken over by large corporations that practice intensive agriculture. Still, there are often small parcels of land in or near suburbs, strips of grass along roads, overgrown or rocky

A fence made of treated wooden posts and galvanized woven wire works best for keeping sheep in a pasture.

pastures, and steep slopes where a few sheep might be grazed for a negligible rent or for no money at all.

Keeping sheep indoors year-round remains an anomaly, although it has been tried in industrialized countries on an experimental basis. The aim is to imitate the intensive methods used with other livestock, but sheep fare best if they can graze. Thus most sheep stay outdoors and are kept in barns only during cold winter weather or for lambing.

The Fenced Pasture

More and more people are beginning to keep only a handful of animals or small flocks of up to perhaps twenty sheep in fenced enclosures. Kept this way, the animals don't need the constant supervision of a shepherd.

Fencing a Pasture

A sturdy, escape-proof fence is essential if you want to keep sheep in a pasture. Sheep wandering into a neighbor's garden are not at all welcome, and fencing is also a prerequisite for keeping dogs out. Of course building and maintaining a fence is expensive and takes work.

Fences made of wood, wire mesh, or woven wire, as well as electric fencing, contain sheep. In some areas stone walls or ditches with water in them work. In most situations, however, a fence made of durable, pressure-treated wooden posts and galvanized woven fencing has proved to be the best solution for at least the outer perimeter of the pasture.

Traditional sheep fencing of woven wire comes in 330 foot rolls and is 3 feet high. The strands are usually closer together at the bottom than at the top to prevent sheep from sticking their heads between the wires and lambs from slipping through. Depending on the soil and the lay of the land, the posts are spaced 6 to 15 feet (2–5 m) apart. When setting the posts it is important to plant them deeply enough to stand firmly. The closer together they are, the less

pressure is exerted on them when the wire is stretched. A good way to brace the fence is to nail or screw cross-rails made of poles or boards to the posts above the woven wire. This not only strengthens the fence but also helps when you stretch the wire from post to post. If your pasture is large, the sheep can make better use of it if you subdivide it into several smaller areas or paddocks. Having at least six paddocks through which the sheep can rotate over the course of the grazing season is most advantageous.

A Lamb Creep

A lamb creep is a device that allows lambs to get at the best grass without interference from adult animals. To make a lamb creep, you build into the fence subdividing the pasture a section of vertical slots wide enough for lambs to squeeze through but too tight for ewes. This way the young, fast-growing lambs can move into a new paddock with fresh grass and pick out the best, tastiest plants. The ewes are let in a week or two later to graze on what is left while the lambs move on to the next paddock. This system has proven very beneficial for the development of lambs. Lamb creeps are also used for giving

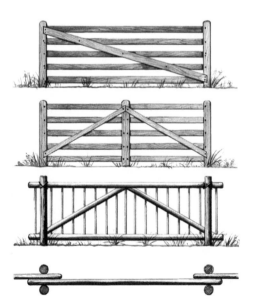

Three kinds of movable wooden fence sections. The upper two have horizontal rails, the third has vertical rungs. The bottom drawing shows in top view how fence sections are attached to posts planted in the ground.

To give lambs a chance to get at the best grass without competition from the bigger sheep, there is a section in the fence where only lambs can get through—the lamb creep.

grain or other supplemental food to lambs in feeders where the ewes cannot get at it.

Management of the Pasture

In temperate zones where the weather changes with the seasons, sheep generally spend the cold part of the year indoors. In the winter and spring taking care of sheep and providing food for them takes up more time. After the winter rest, pastures may have to be fertilized in early spring, piles of earth spread, and fences checked and mended. Don't, however, overfertilize a pasture. Generally a moderate amount of phosphorus and potassium added to composted sheep manure is sufficient. A pasture treated with such compost grows a variety of plants that are both tasty and wholesome and that provide forage superior to the lush growth resulting from excessive nitrogen fertilization. I don't mean to deny that enormous crop increases can sometimes be achieved by applying nitrogen fertilizer or to denigrate the products of the chemical industry. If you can afford to pass up production increases that depend on commercial nitrogen fertilizers, however, I recommend your doing so for environmental reasons. Many plants that grew commonly in meadows and fields have become rare or are endangered, largely on account of the widespread use of nitrogen fertilizers and herbicides.

Depending on weather and temperature, sheep can be put out to pasture sometime between March and May when the new grass averages about 2 to 3 inches in height. In the interest of maximizing the yield of the pasture, sheep should not be let out too early because otherwise they graze the paddocks bare too quickly one after the other. It is better to supplement the fresh grass with hay and feed at first and not to open up all the paddocks too soon. The yield of a pasture depends not only on the weather and the quality of the soil but just as much on well-planned use. A pasture produces best if it is grazed intensively but briefly and then left to rest for some time. This rest period also helps control parasites (see pages 39–41).

For this reason and also to preserve a desirable variety of forage plants, rotation between grazing and hay or silage production is highly recommended. A similar beneficial effect is achieved by letting different kinds of animals, such as sheep, cattle, horses, pigs, and geese, use the same pasture, either together or in succession. Sheep and horses complement each other quite well. Pastures used exclusively by horses deteriorate because of the increasingly rank growth around the piles of horse manure. Sheep eat these plants, making use of food that would otherwise go to waste. At the same time they improve the pasture and interrupt the reproductive cycle of horse parasites. Horses, in turn, graze happily in areas fertilized with sheep dung and discourage the parasites to which sheep are subject. (There is only one kind of intestinal worm that thrives equally well in both kinds of hosts.)

Assuming the animals are used to each other, sheep and horses can be kept together on the same pasture. Only at lambing time should the ewes and their lambs be kept separate from the horses. Otherwise there is a danger that the lambs may accidentally be stepped on and crushed by the horses.

How Many Sheep on How Much Pasture?

The proper relationship between the number of animals and the amount of land needed for them (the stocking rate) depends largely on soil fertility, climate, and how intensively the pasture is managed (fertilizing, and length of pasturing and rest periods). An acre of good pasture can support three to five ewes with their lambs, assuming the lambs are slaughtered or sold when they weigh about 90 pounds (40 kg). The land is not only grazed but also produces hay for winter. This is merely a rough general estimate, however. On a fertile, intensively managed pasture—this means that two to ten days of grazing are alternated with twenty to forty days of rest for the grass to grow back and that the land is heavily fertilized or the animals are given supplemental feed—the number of animals can be increased. On the other hand, if the sheep graze the same pasture all year round, if the soil is poor and no fertilizer is applied, if the climate is unfavorable, and if the sheep receive no supplemental feed, even three ewes per acre is too many.

Letting sheep graze continually on the same pasture is the least economical method of keeping sheep. On the other hand, it also requires the least amount of labor and, for someone with plenty of land but little time who can spend only few, irregular hours looking after the sheep, it can be a good solution. Under these conditions, however, the stocking rate must be reduced, that is, fewer animals can be kept on the same area of pasture.

Someone with enough time to manage sheep intensively and use the pasture optimally can increase yields by increasing the number of animals per acre.

Movable Pens and Tethering

One way to let single animals (especially milk sheep) graze is to tether them. For this purpose you put a leather collar on the animal and hook a light metal chain about 6 to 12 feet (2–4 m) long to it. The other end of the chain is attached by means of a ring to a peg that is sunk *all the way* into the earth. It is important to include a swivel link at each end of the chain so that the chain can't become twisted and the animal can't strangle itself on it. You must also make sure that there is nothing within the radius of the chain on which the chain could become entangled. Even small shrubs and fallen or low-hanging tree branches can become dangerous. If you tether more than one sheep, you must make sure, of course, that their ranges don't overlap. Otherwise they may accidentally choke each other with their chains. When you tether a sheep for the first time you should watch it for awhile until it has adjusted to its new situation. Tethered sheep must be given water regularly and brought home if the weather is very bad (excessive heat or heavy downpours).

You can let a single sheep graze by tethering it. Put a leather collar on the animal, and clasp a light metal chain 10 to 12 feet long (3–4 m) to it. Attach the other end of the chain to a peg that is sunk all the way into the earth.

Tethering makes it possible to use tiny areas and sometimes even the banks of country roads for grazing.

Another way to let sheep graze new grass every day and at the same time give them more freedom of movement is to use a movable pen. Such a pen can consist of a light, temporary electric fence attached to posts that can be put up and taken down quickly and easily. Starting at one corner, you move some of the posts every day in such a way that a new strip of grass of the right size for the needs of the animals is made available for grazing. Part of the already grazed area is enclosed by the fence and is used by the sheep for moving around, resting, and defecating; the section that lies outside the fence can recover and start growing fresh grass. With a movable pen of this sort, optimal use can be made of a pasture and the risk of parasite infestation kept to a minimum at the same time.

The Barn

Larger flocks of sheep are usually housed in large, subdivided sheds or open barns during the winter. If you have only a few sheep, you can house them in an old, empty sheep shed, barn, or other outbuilding. If there is no old building available, an open shelter erected on the pasture will do.

Shelter and Barn Space

A shelter should always be large enough to accommodate all the animals comfortably. You should figure on about 12 to 15 square feet (1.2–1.5m²) for each mature breeding ewe and on 5 to 8 square feet (0.5–0.8m²) per lamb. It does no harm if the animals have more space.

Choose as dry a site as possible for erecting a shelter on a pasture; the structure should never be located where rain accumulates after a lengthy rainfall. The shelter should have a solid wall on the side where most of the bad weather (wind and rain) comes from and be open on the opposite side. To keep the wooden parts near the ground from rotting too quickly, you can rest the corner posts on a footing of rocks or dig treated posts (similar to telephone poles) into the ground as corner posts.

The barn area where the sheep spend extended periods of time should be dry and receive plenty of light. A temperature of 43 to 57° F (6–14° C) with a relative air humidity of 60 to 80% seems to be ideal for sheep. Sheep are even more sensitive to warm, moist barn air than other livestock; therefore the ceiling should, if at all possible, be at least 12 feet (4 m) high and, if the number of animals is small, the floor area per sheep should not be less than 15 square feet. A barn that is used for housing sheep should also have a window area that is about 1/15 the floor area. The doors should always open to the outside and preferably be mounted in such a way that they can be replaced easily with doors made up of slats that allow the air to circulate better when it gets warm. The air exchange should start in the barn, however, and drafts should always be avoided.

Bedding

Straw is most commonly used for bedding, and through the repeated addition of new layers a solid "mattress" gradually builds up. Make sure that this deep bedding always remains dry. If you use this kind of deep bedding, it is a good idea to raise the feeding troughs and hay racks to adjust to the mounting surface of the bedding. When the sheep move out to pasture, the bedding is cleaned out along with the manure. Cleaning out a barn is an unpleasant and sweaty job if you have to do it by hand with a pitchfork. A front loader does the job in no time and is of great help, particularly if you have a large number of animals, but the barn must be built to accommodate the machine.

Sheep can also be kept on slatted floors without bedding. Such a floor can be made of wooden planks about 1 inch (2 cm) apart or of commercially manufactured metal racks. The owner of only a few sheep is unlikely to opt for this method, however, which is probably also considerably less appealing to the animals.

Lambing Pens

If you have quite a few sheep you may want to subdivide the barn space with movable wooden fence sections (see drawing on page 19) into several compartments. You should in any case set up lambing pens for ewes that are getting ready to lamb. The ewes and the newborn lambs can then spend the first few days together undisturbed in the pens until the bond between mother and lamb is well established and the new lambs have gained some strength and lost their initial awkwardness.

Hayracks and Grain Feeders

The advantages of feeders and hayracks are that the feed offered in them stays clean, each animal can be given its proper ration, and very little feed is wasted by becoming lost in the bedding. You can give your sheep hay in a hayrack mounted on a wall and grain in a troughlike feeder made of wood, metal, or glazed clay. A more efficient method is to combine the two in one structure, with the feeding trough below the hayrack. This way, the small bits of hay, grass seeds, and broken grass leaves that fall

Care and Maintenance

A good feeder is important for proper food intake. It should be constructed in a way that keeps the food clean, allows each animal to get at its ration, and prevents waste of food through spilling.

between the slats of the rack collect in the trough, where they can still be eaten by the sheep. By designing the feeder so that the slanted slats of the hayrack are above the feeding trough, you can keep the sheep from jumping into the trough and dirtying or spilling the grain. To keep hay from falling on the necks and backs of the sheep from the upper part of the hayrack and soiling the wool, you can nail up some boards at the appropriate places. The feeders should accommodate whatever kind of feed you use and be as space saving as possible. Keeping these points in mind, you can build feeders yourself to fit your particular needs. You can also buy commercially made feeding racks and troughs designed for sheep. If you plan to use them, figure on a length of 24 to 28 inches (60–70 cm) per ewe with her offspring. The space between the slats of the hayrack should be about 2 inches (5 cm) so that only small mouthfuls of hay are pulled out that are then eaten up right away. Hayracks and feeders can be attached to the barn walls or set up freestanding, back to back. Freestanding feeders take up more space, but they can be moved to wherever they are needed, and since the sheep eat on both sides, they accommodate twice the number of animals.

Storage Space for Hay and Straw

If you keep your sheep on straw bedding and feed them primarily on hay, you will need about 20 to 30 cubic feet (2–3 m³) of storage space per animal. The most convenient place to store hay and straw is a hayloft above the animals, but there should always be a solid wall or ceiling between the hay and the animals. Otherwise the vapors emanating from the sheep may encourage the growth of molds and other organisms that spoil the hay. If other storage buildings are available, those closest to the barn are of course most practical. Just remember that hay and straw should not be stored directly on the ground. Place a wooden rack about 1 foot high under it, and also check that the roof overhead is not leaking.

If necessary you can store hay and straw outdoors. Make sure it does not rest directly on the ground, and cover it carefully with plastic tarpaulins, securing them well against wind and rain.

The same principle of dry storage on a wooden floor applies to grain and other concentrated feeds. For some kinds of feeds, a silo may be appropriate. Moisture spoils stored feed, lowers its nutritional value, and may possibly lead to poisoning if molds and bacteria produce toxins and other products of decomposition.

Identification Marks

A permanent mark of identification helps in recognizing individual sheep and keeping track of their age and breeding performance. If you have a flock of registered sheep, identification marks are a prerequisite. The identification mark generally consists of a number that is tattooed into the animal's ear. This method is preferable to fastening metal tags to the ears because the tags can cause infections and are often ripped out.

For short-term identification, as when an animal requires treatment or when two or more flocks are temporarily combined, a mark on the fleece with spray paint or with large, appropriately colored marking crayons is generally sufficient to differentiate them.

Care and Maintenance

Necessary Care

Trimming Hoofs (see drawing on page 41)

How often a sheep's hoofs need trimming depends on the consistency of the ground and on how fast the hoofs grow. Trimming should be done at least twice a year, however: before the animals are put out to pasture in the spring and again in the late fall. Set the sheep down on its rump in front of you so that you can work without the animal struggling. Trim the hoofs to their proper length with a sharp hoof knife. The feet must also be examined for changes and irregularities. Healthy hoofs need only have the tips trimmed and the edges, which are often rolled under, cut back enough so that the animal supports its weight on the cut edge of the horn when walking on solid, level ground. Hollow pockets and rotten spots in the horn need to be cut out deeply.

It is probably best if you have a shepherd show you how to trim a sheep's feet the first time; afterward you can perform this simple task yourself. If bleeding results from the cutting, you should apply an antibacterial spray to the cut immediately. Bandaging is usually unnecessary because the bleeding is not likely to last long.

Shearing

All wool sheep must be sheared (see color photo on page 56) once a year. Shearing is done primarily for the sake of using the sheep's wool but also to relieve the animal of its thick coat in the hot summer and to prevent matting and parasite infestations.

The best time to shear sheep is at the onset of warm weather, usually in late April or early May. Choose a warm, sunny day. If the animals suffer from ectoparasites (see page 39), treatment is easy to administer shortly after shearing.

If you hope to obtain clean wool of good quality, your sheep must be kept clean. Dung caked in the wool or bits of hay or bedding worked into it considerably lower the value of a fleece.

Sheep should be dry when they are about to be shorn. Experienced shearers set the animal down on its haunches the same way as when trimming the hoofs and proceed to shear evenly from the head back and from the belly up to the back until the fleece falls off in a single piece. There may be people who are able to do a decent job of shearing with hand shears (the type that is closed by force of the hand and opens again by spring action), but an electric shearing machine makes the work a lot easier. Electric shears allow you to work quickly and neatly and reduce the danger of nicking the skin. The shearing head should always be kept very sharp so that it slices the wool off smoothly, the setting screw must be tight, and the machine should be oiled before you start using it. If you check these three items, shearing should give you no problems. To avoid nicking the animal, stretch the skin slightly. This gives you a flat surface to shear and prevents the skin from forming folds. Never pull on the wool because this causes folds. When you work along the natural skin folds in the throat, leg, and tail areas, special caution is in order.

In rams the scrotal region and in ewes the vulva require special attention so that they are not injured. Even with the most careful handling, however, skin injuries cannot always be avoided. If you promptly apply tincture of iodine or an antibiotic spray, the cut will generally heal quickly and without any further complications.

If you have only a few sheep and don't own a shearing machine, you can ask a sheep farmer or a professional shearer to shear your animals. With today's prices, however, the wool alone is usually not enough compensation for the job. The wool should be sorted and stored in bags immediately after shearing.

Feeding Sheep Right

What and How Much Food Do Sheep Need?

Sheep are grazing animals, and the plants growing on a pasture are what they are naturally adapted to consume.

Every organism needs protein to sustain itself and carbohydrates to supply the energy needed for its activities. Minerals, trace elements, and vitamins are also needed, and water is a basic requirement for all life processes.

When you buy feed, the amount of digestible protein is usually indicated in percentage figures, and the carbohydrate contents in units of pure carbohydrates (1 unit is the amount of energy supplied by 1 g of pure carbohydrate). The fiber content (plant cellulose) is also often indicated in percentages. A ewe with a lamb needs about 4 pounds (1.8 kg) of dry feed containing at least 5½ ounces (155 g) of protein and 800 units of pure carbohydrates.

There are different methods of feeding sheep during the winter, and the choice of one of them depends mostly on the availability and cost of various kinds of feed. *Sheep should always have sufficient water, hay for eating, and a mineral salt block for licking.* If you give your sheep nothing but hay, you should figure on about 3½ to 5½ pounds (1.7–2.5 kg) per day per breeding animal. If you supplement the hay with 1 to 1½ pounds (500–700 g) of grain, you can cut down on the hay to about 3 pounds (1.5 kg). Hay consumption also drops if you supplement hay with silage or turnips. The best way to meet the added nutritional demands of ewes toward the end of pregnancy, of ewes with new lambs, and of fast-growing market lambs is to feed the animals more grain.

The best way to determine whether the sheep are receiving the right amount of food is to examine them. If they keep becoming fatter, it is time to cut down on their ration, and if they are losing weight and becoming scrawny, they should get more to eat. Of course, a proper assessment of their condition requires some experience. A sheep with a thick coat of wool may give a false visual impression. You must use your hands and feel the animal's back to see if it is covered with a layer of fat or if the spine and hip bones are sticking out. If you have only a few sheep, a commercial feed blend for breeding animals is practical.

Hay and Straw

Hay remains the basic staple of sheep during winter and whenever they are kept inside. Hay is simply field or meadow grasses preserved through drying. Several factors affect the quality and nutritional value of hay.

First, the quality of hay depends on the varieties and proportions of grasses and other herbaceous plants that make up the hay. A hayfield that has been overfertilized with nitrogen (manure and sludge) and consequently has turned into a monoculture of a few kinds of grasses (foxtail, quackgrass, and orchard grass) does not make good hay. A plant community that includes many different feed grasses and clovers, as well as other plants (dandelions, vetches, acanthus, plantain, cinquefoils, and others) makes for good and palatable hay that practically eliminates the need for supplementary feeds during winter.

The growth stage of the grass when it is cut is also of crucial importance for the nutritional quality of hay, particularly for its protein content. The younger the grass, the more protein and the less fiber it contains. The food value of a given amount of hay consisting of young grass is considerably higher than that of the same amount of hay that was cut when the grass was in full bloom or even later in the summer and therefore is made up mostly of tough plant stems and withered grass leaves. Grass that is mowed prematurely, on the other hand, does not produce a good yield and dries badly. The best time to cut grass is during its early bloom (end of May to June in temperate latitudes).

In addition to the composition and age of the

Feeding Sheep Right

plants making up the hay, the way it is dried and especially the "haying weather" significantly affect quality. Good hay should be brought under cover within three to four days after mowing and should preferably not have been rained on. The longer hay lies on the hayfield, the poorer the quality of the hay as more earth is mixed into it by the haying machines and exposure to moisture is greater.

If you have only a couple of animals and plenty of time, you can mow a meadow by hand with a scythe, the way it used to be done. Some people get real pleasure from scything and seeing the mowed grass lying there in neat windrows. Most sheep owners want to use mechanized equipment (a tractor with a mowing bar or a rotary mower) to save time. If the weather is good, the mowed grass must be fluffed and turned in the morning after the dew dries off and again in the afternoon so that it dries well and evenly. If it doesn't rain, the hay is usually ready for bringing in after three days and can be stored for winter in a dry, covered place. If the weather looks unpredictable, drying the hay on wooden racks is a good but labor-intensive method. Hay that is baled is easier to transport, store, and measure out.

After the hay is harvested, it goes through a ripening process that is accompanied by heating and further evaporation of water; the hay "sweats." Hay should not be fed to the animals until this process is fully completed, that is, about ten to twelve weeks after harvest.

If hay contains too much moisture when it is brought in, the heat it develops may be so great that there is danger of combustion. In addition, valuable nutritional substances are destroyed, and molds develop. Hay that is several years old loses more and more of its food value, with the vitamin content beginning to deteriorate even toward the end of the first winter.

Many people with only a couple of sheep buy their winter's supply of hay in bales from a farmer or hay dealer. If you have enough storage space, it is more advantageous to buy your hay on the field directly from the farmer because you have the chance to choose first-quality hay and you may be able to buy it at a better price.

Good hay looks green and is not made up primarily of tough grass stalks but also contains many fine grass leaves and leaves of various other herbaceous plants. It has a pleasant, aromatic smell. Hay that looks brownish usually has been rained on too much and has less food value. If dust rises when the hay is shaken, if it smells musty, or if you see spots of mold or rot, the hay should not be fed to the animals because it can cause illness (see page 42).

Straw is also used to feed sheep. It should always be clean, dried thoroughly, and free of fungi. Sheep, as ruminants, are able to derive energy even from the stems of grain (straw), which have only minimal food value. Sheep should be given as much straw as they will eat in addition to their normal ration of hay, silage, turnips, and concentrated feed. Straw from barley and oats is best for this purpose; straw from wheat and rye is less suitable.

Silage

Silage can be made from freshly mown grass, the tops of root vegetables, or chopped corn. These foods are preserved by undergoing a chemical fermentation process in the airtight environment of a silo. For someone with only a few sheep, making one's own silage is generally out of the question because of the cost of producing it. Silage that is in perfect condition, clean and fresh, can be given to sheep, but sheep are particularly susceptible to listeriosis (see page 43), a disease caused by bacteria found in spoiled or dirty silage. If you want to feed your sheep mostly silage, you can give each animal between 5 and 8 pounds (2.5–4 kg) per day, but you should always give some hay along with the silage.

Mountain pastures: A flock of sheep are returning from their summer pasture in the mountains to the valley.

26

Feeding Sheep Right

Turnips, Carrots, and Potatoes

In the old days every farmer planted a field of turnips. Turnips are nutritious and readily eaten by livestock. Today hardly anybody plants turnips for animal feed because planting turnips requires too much labor, even with the help of modern machinery. If you have a large garden or a small field and some spare time, planting turnips or carrots as winter feed is still worthwhile, or you may be able to buy some for winter from a truck farm. Turnips that are harvested in the fall must be stored in a cellar or root cellar where the temperature stays above freezing. In the winter about 2/3 pounds (300 g) of clean turnips, whole or cut up, can be given along with the hay.

Dried sugar beet chips can be fed to sheep the same way as turnips. They are a by-product of the sugar industry and are sold as is or in pellet form in 100-pound bags. They can be soaked in water before being fed to the sheep, or small amounts (1/3 pound, 150 g, per animal) can be given dry. Sheep also eat potatoes and potato peelings either raw or cooked. Because potatoes are high in carbohydrates they are considered a high-energy food.

Concentrated Feeds

Concentrated feeds are high in energy and protein, easily digestible, and used primarily for animals with higher than usual nutritional needs (ewes in late pregnancy, ewes with twin lambs, lambs being fattened for market, and breeding rams).

Regional breeds with horns:
Above, left: Gray, horned Heidschnucke ram from the author's stock (the Heidschnucke, practically unknown in the U.S.A., generally gives birth to single lambs); above, right: Mouflon ram; below, left: Gray, horned Heidschnucke with her newborn lamb, which are always coal black at birth; below, right: English four-horned sheep after shearing.

Grain is an important basic ingredient of concentrated foods. Sheep are able to chew and digest unmilled oat and barley grain. Concentrated feeds often include cracked grain, wheat bran, and cracked soybeans. Cracked soybeans are an excellent source of protein, but they are rather expensive.

In recent years feed mixtures have gained in importance. The feed industry produces livestock feed, usually in pellet form, from a variety of components. In addition to feed mixtures for breeding and for young animals, there is also a special finishing ration to fatten lambs for market. These commercial feed mixtures are composed to meet the animals' needs for protein, energy, minerals, and vitamins as established through scientific research.

In addition to feed mixtures designed for sheep, some cattle feeds can be used as sheep food.

Using feed mixtures simplifies the feeding of the animals and prevents nutritional deficiencies, and compared with feeds consisting of a single kind of feed, such as rye meal or dried sugar beets, feed mixtures are usually fairly inexpensive.

Water

When sheep are *out on the pasture*, how much water they need a day depends a great deal on the amount of precipitation and on the water content of the forage. Milking sheep need more water than other sheep. When the grass is fresh and juicy in the spring and if there is sufficient rainfall, sheep need hardly any additional drinking water. You should therefore not be alarmed if they refuse to drink the water you give them. Nevertheless, sheep should always have water available. A stream or automatic waterer is ideal, but a tub or bucket that is always full of fresh water will do perfectly well.

In winter sheep need about 2 quarts (2 liters) of water a day. In principle, they should always have as much drinking water available as they want, in winter as well as in summer. Wash the water buckets or tubs every day, and refill them with fresh water. Place them where they cannot be kicked over and—equally important—where the water is not likely to be contaminated with dung.

There are automatic waterers for sheep; some are activated by the animals when they press against them, and others are equipped with floats that maintain a steady water level (similar to the device in toilet tanks). Waterers must be checked regularly for cleanliness and functionability. It is also important to keep the water in them from freezing during cold winter weather.

Breeding and Raising Sheep

Purebred and Crossbred Sheep

A *breed* is characterized by certain traits that are common to its members and that distinguish them from other animals of the same species. To preserve the breed and encourage its evolution in the direction of specific goals, it is necessary that the breeding stock be selected by human beings.

Registered sheep represent the highest level of breeding purebred sheep as practiced in modern, highly civilized countries. All breeding stock is marked, recorded, and bred according to accepted standards under the supervision of official breeders' organizations.

Selective breeding of purebred sheep, whether with registered or unregistered stock, is crucial for the preservation of the various breeds, their particular genetic makeup, and their special qualities and appearance. Selective breeding also has advantages for the owner of a few animals because he or she can choose the kind of sheep that suit the situation best and can keep some of his or her own lambs as breeding stock.

In addition to purebred sheep, there are also planned and unplanned *crosses*. In planned crossbreeding, the breeder makes use of the heterosis effect (greater vigor, and better achievements) that characterizes lambs with parents of different breeds. These hybrid lambs are usually not used for further breeding but are slaughtered. Unplanned crosses are rather common in flocks of only a few animals. Crossings of mountain sheep with merinos and of black-faced sheep with milk sheep are examples, and the offspring are often used for further breeding. These matings are usually more the result of chance than of breeding plans, and after a while the sheep, although clearly different from wild sheep, can no longer be assigned to a particular breed.

The *Corriedale* is a crossbred wool sheep developed in New Zealand during the 1880's. Other popular crossbred wool breeds include the *Columbia* and the *Targhee*, both of which were developed in the western regions of the United States.

During the breeding season sheep indicate their readiness to mate through certain gestures: When a ewe urinates, an interested ram often pulls back his upper lip in a characteristic expression.

Estrus

Sheep breeds with seasonal estrus go into heat only once a year, in the fall. The so-called out-of-season breeders may start the sexual cycle any time of the year. Seasonal estrus begins in the fall when the days begin to shorten and subsides in the spring when the days lengthen again. If a ewe in heat is not impregnated, the next heat period comes after 17 to 20 days (estrus cycle). The period of receptivity is about 24 hours. Although regional breeds, meat sheep, and milk sheep come into heat only in the fall and drop their lambs in the spring, mountain sheep and merino sheep can start the breeding cycle and have lambs any time of the year. Black-faced meat ewes go into heat in the fall, but they can be bred at other times of the year as well.

The breeding season usually starts in September or October. At this time the ram is brought together with the ewes for the breeding period. A one-year-old ram can handle at most thirty, an older ram fifty to sixty ewes. If you have only a few sheep or a single ewe, keeping a breeding ram is not economical. It is not easy to tell whether a ewe is in heat. If

Breeding and Raising Sheep

you are not sure, the best thing to do is to take your ewes to the owner of a ram who will let your ewes join his or her flock for a while.

One method that has proven successful is to feed the ewes sparingly for about two weeks in August, after they have been wormed and before the breeding season sets in. The ewes should be put on a meager pasture or on one that has already been partially grazed by lambs, and they should not be given supplementary minerals or grain. Then, when they are brought into a lush pasture together with the ram and are given minerals and grain again, they go into heat quickly and almost simultaneously. The number of embryos started is very high, and most of the lambs are born within a few days in the spring.

If you don't have enough time to devote to your sheep during the lambing period in the winter, it is better if the lambs are not born until the end of April or early May. At this time of year, the external conditions are much more favorable for the baby animals than in the earlier months, and lambs at this point easily survive being born in an open shelter on the pasture. By late fall they will still be big enough to be sold for slaughter. Since the ewes have fresh, protein-rich grass to eat by May, you can do without expensive grain rations. If you want your lambs not to be born until this favorable springtime, you must keep your ewes away from the ram in the fall (also from uncastrated ram lambs!). Don't let the ram join the ewes before December. Some shepherds temporarily put a kind of apron on the breeding ram to prevent him from impregnating ewes at the wrong time.

Your goals will be quite different if you have milk sheep and would like to have fresh milk for as much of the year as possible. In this case you want to stagger the breeding of your ewes. If you have three ewes, for instance, you may want to breed the first one as early as August, the second one toward the end of October, and the last not until December or January. This way you will have a freshening ewe several times a year (a milk animal freshens when the milk begins to flow after the birth of her young).

Some sheep owners with only a few animals solve the problem of reproduction differently. They raise a good, strong, uncastrated ram lamb in the spring (February or March) whose mother has the desired traits, such as high milk production, good conversion of feed, and a tendency to multiple births. Such a lamb can also be bought or bartered from another sheep breeder. This ram lamb impregnates the ewes in the fall and is slaughtered afterward in the late fall or during the winter. This method is quite economical, but it runs counter to the rules of selective breeding.

Lambing

Difficult and abnormal births are much rarer among sheep than among cattle and pigs, which are intensively managed and dependent on human care. This is especially true of sheep kept under a low-input system, grazing in flocks on pastures and often lambing without human assistence. Among the different sheep breeds, the older regional breeds, such as the mountain sheep and the German Heidschnucke, hardly ever need human intervention when lambing because they have retained their hardy constitution and strong mothering instinct. Highly productive meat breeds are more likely to need assistance when giving birth and require greater care for some time afterward.

After a gestation period of 145 to 155 days (five months), a ewe gives birth to one or more lambs. Ewes of older breeds and ewes lambing for the first time often have single lambs; twin births are quite frequent in most breeds developed for productivity. In terms of profitability, twin births are, of course, desirable. In some exceptionally prolific breeds, ewes sometimes even have triplets or quadruplets. Such multiple births are more common in milk sheep, however.

It is advisable, especially if you have quite a few sheep (more than three ewes), to move ewes that are getting ready to lamb into separate, clean lambing pens, where they can give birth and become acquainted with their newborn lambs undisturbed.

Breeding and Raising Sheep

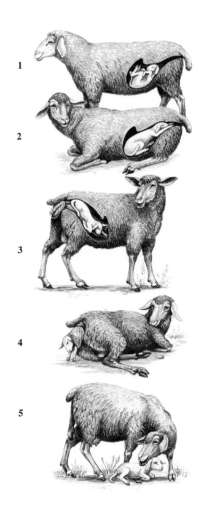

The birth of a lamb:
1 Position of the fetus toward the end of gestation
2 Normal birth position
3 Position for hindfeet coming first
4 The lamb is expelled by the force of uterine contractions
5 The mother licks the newborn dry; she has not yet passed the afterbirth

The swelling of the udder and a slackening and softening of the vulva are outward signs of the approaching birth.

The birth process itself, after the lengthy preparatory period, can be divided into three phases:

• the opening up phase, when the birth canal gradually widens
• the expulsion phase, during which the lamb is pushed out through the birth canal by a series of strong contractions
• the afterbirth phase, when the uterus rids itself of the placenta and of fetal membranes

A normal birth takes anywhere from one-half to two hours. You should never interfere in a normal lambing but leave the ewe undisturbed in a quiet, clean spot. The normal position of a lamb ready to be born is with its spine upward toward the ewe's spine and with its head and front legs pointed toward the vagina. There are many variations of this position, most of which present no problem. However, there are certain positions that can be fatal for either the lamb or the ewe if they are not corrected properly. These include the following:

• an abnormal position of the lamb
• insufficient dilation of the cervix
• multiple lambs that get in each other's way in the birth canal
• lambs that are too large

However, the great majority of lambings proceed smoothly without help from humans. If you observe abnormal behavior in the ewe or if the birthing process seems to take too long, it is best for a new sheep owner to call a veterinarian or an experienced sheep person in good time.

The newborn lamb should drink the first milk produced by the ewe (the colostrum) *as soon as possible*. The colostrum supplies the lamb with energy and loosens the first tarry feces. It also contains antibodies that help the lamb fight off diseases at this early stage of life.

Breeding and Raising Sheep

A lamb weighs about 5 to 10% of its mother's weight at birth. Like all plant-eating herd animals, lambs are born fully developed and able to stand up, find their mother's teats, and nurse unaided within a few minutes after birth. Ewes with a good mothering instinct immediately start licking their lambs all over and guiding them to their milk-filled udders for nursing. In a harsh local environment or during bad weather this mothering instinct is of crucial importance for the survival of newborn lambs. I have seen a ewe of mixed breed give birth to twin lambs on an open pasture covered with deep snow on a winter night when the temperature dropped to -5° F (-20°C). In the morning both lambs were happily running through the snow behind their mother, thanks to their mother's care and their own hardy constitution. It is better if the lambing does not have to take place outdoors in below-freezing weather, however. Highly bred lambs of breeds developed for productivity often fail to survive under such conditions, especially if the ewe lacks a good mothering instinct. Young lambs fare best if the pregnant ewe is placed in a lambing pen before giving birth. Then, when the lambs are a few days old and the mother-child bond is well established, both ewe and offspring can rejoin the flock.

Dangers to Newborn Lambs

Birth and the first few days of life are fraught with danger for young lambs. If they survive the birth, the baby lambs, which are rather clumsy during their first few hours of life, then face the hazards of an unfamiliar and not always hospitable world. A lamb born during cold, wet weather and in the midst of a flock may not be accepted by its mother (particularly in multiple births). If it fails to get its mother's colostrum and wanders around lost, it may succumb to weakness and cold or be crushed to death.

Lambs born in a barn or in a makeshift lambing pen can get lost, too. If they wander about lost, they may become stuck in old equipment that is lying around, or they may drown in a tub of water. Inju-

ries inflicted by other animals, such as sheep, billy goats, dogs, or horses, may also lead to death (see page 43).

I don't mean to suggest that raising lambs is so hazardous that it is practically impossible. If you take good care of your animals, and especially if you don't have too many, situations like the ones mentioned are very rare. They can usually be avoided if you watch out for them and take the proper precautions.

Nursing lambs wiggle their tails; this stimulates the mother to sniff the lamb's anal region.

Raising Lambs

A Lamb with Its Mother

If you have only a few sheep, you can leave the ewes and their lambs together in the pasture until the lambs are ready for market. This system requires the least labor. Creep feeding, supplemental grain rations, and worming all help the lambs grow faster. Lambs that are not needed for breeding should be sold or slaughtered before the breeding cycle starts again but at the very latest in the early fall when forage becomes sparser. Special methods of fattening the lambs, which often involve weaning the lambs early, are generally used only in large sheep operations.

Breeding and Raising Sheep

Raising a Lamb with an Adoptive Mother

Some ewes have more than one lamb, and sometimes a ewe dies during or shortly after giving birth. There are also ewes whose lambs don't survive birth or the first few days of life. One or two orphaned lambs can usually be "grafted" to such a lambless ewe.

In most cases it is rather difficult to get a ewe to accept a strange lamb. The orphaned lamb is best introduced right after the ewe has given birth and while the stillborn lamb is still wet. The orphaned lamb is rubbed against the ewe's natural lamb to become smeared with its birth fluids (slime grafting), or the dead lamb can be skinned and the pelt wrapped around the orphaned lamb (skin grafting) so that the ewe will identify it as her own by its odor. During the first few days it is usually necessary to restrain the ewe so that she will hold still when the adoptive lamb wants to nurse.

Bottle-feeding a Lamb

If no adoptive mother is available to raise an orphaned lamb, it can be bottle-fed. This can be a rewarding experience if you have enough time (see color photo, above, right, on back cover). Bottle-fed lambs become very attached to humans and follow them everywhere. If you take your time and the cost of food into account, however, artificial rearing of lambs is very uneconomical. This is why many commercial sheep operators dispose of third lambs or lambs of very young ewes. Often you can get them for free.

If at all possible, any lamb that is to be bottle-fed should get at least some colostrum from its mother. Sheep's milk, milk replacer (available at feed stores), or cow's milk can be used for bottle-feeding, and regular vitamin supplements are recommended. You can introduce motherless lambs quite early to commercial lamb feed in pellet form and to good hay. The success of rearing orphaned lambs also depends on cleanliness, a regular feeding schedule, and prompt treatment by a veterinarian at the first sign of sickness, such as diarrhea.

You can use a normal baby bottle and rubber nipple for a lamb. Longish nipples work best. Enlarge the hole in the nipple somewhat, but don't make it so large that the lamb chokes on too much milk. At the beginning you must feed the lamb as frequently as possible, giving it small amounts of milk heated to body temperature five or six times a day. Later two or three larger feedings are adequate. By the time the lamb is eight weeks old, it should have changed to eating grass, hay, and grain by itself. The artificial rearing of a number of orphaned lambs can turn out to be economical, unlike bottle-feeding a single lamb. In such a situation, a

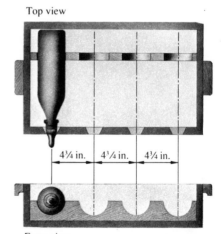

Top view

Front view

4¼ in. 4¼ in. 4¼ in.

Cross section

Diagrams of a four-bottle lamb bar that you can build yourself (top view, front view, and cross section). You can use ordinary baby bottles with rubber nipples.

Breeding and Raising Sheep

lamb bar is set up, which consists of a bucket with several nipples. Commercial lamb starter is used. Lambs can survive on a diet made up exclusively of solid food by the time they are three weeks old. Of course, this first food should be as palatable, easily digestible, and nutritious as possible.

Castrating and Docking Lambs

All ram lambs that are not going to be separated from the rest of the flock (sold or slaughtered) by the time they are three to five months old should be castrated before they are more than a couple of weeks old. Young, uncastrated rams disturb the flock's peace with their excess energy, and they may also engage in unplanned and undesirable matings. Castration is best performed by a veterinarian, who is the only one qualified to administer the anethesia that my be necessary.

Lambs that belong to long-tailed breeds and are later to be used as breeding stock usually have their tails docked (removed). This is to prevent the accumulation of manure and urine on their hindquarters. This operation can be performed either with a knife or bloodlessly with a rubber ring. This, too, if it is going to be done at all, should be performed as early as possible. The tails of ewe lambs should not be cut too short; the stub should be long enough to cover the vulva.

In any event, check local animal protection regulations, the intent of which is to prevent accidents and cruelty to animals by requiring that only qualified persons treat animals and slaughter them.

Since sheep are very susceptible to tetanus infections, everything must be absolutely clean for these operations, and an antibacterial powder or spray should be applied. If tetanus has occurred in your flock, a veterinarian may recommend additional precautions, such as giving antibiotic serum or giving the ewes tetanus shots.

Young lambs at play: Some of their spare energy finds expression in wild chases and in leaps into the air, with all four feet leaving the ground at once.

If Your Sheep Get Sick

General Remarks

Shepherds have traditionally spent much of their lives with their animals and thus were able to acquire considerable expertise in treating the sicknesses of sheep. They have always had a popular reputation for being close to nature and having special knowledge of nature's cures, and the right of the shepherd to treat the flock derives from this history. In many cases methods of treatment based on experience and old lore work well, but some widespread old treatments are no longer defensible in view of the advances in knowledge and the techniques available today. There are now highly effective drugs against infectious diseases and parasites. Most of these drugs require prescriptions and can be legally obtained only through a veterinarian who supervises their use.

If you are a novice shepherd, you should seek professional advice when problems arise. If sheep or lambs die, an autopsy can often reveal the cause of death, thus making it possible to initiate proper treatment for the rest of the flock or to institute prophylactic measures.

Prevention

The key to having healthy and strong animals is to keep them in a sanitary environment and to provide good and knowledgeable care for them.

One very important requirement is to prevent pathogens, especially parasites, from establishing themselves in the barn and on the pasture. Once they become established, they can quickly spread to a dangerous degree.

If you feed your sheep the right amounts of a diet that meets all their nutritional needs and if you check the appearance and behavior of your animals, sickness is not likely to become a serious problem.

Above: A lamb jumping across a brook. Below: A battle of rivalry; two males are ramming their heads together.

Parasites and Harmful Insects

External Parasites (Ectoparasites)

Sheep keds (*Melophagus ovinus*) are a widespread pest among sheep. These wingless, blackish brown flies feed on their host's blood and bother the sheep by crawling around on the skin underneath the fleece. Sheep keds produce larvae at the pupal stage. Since sheep often crowd together, this parasite easily spreads by crawling from one animal to the next.

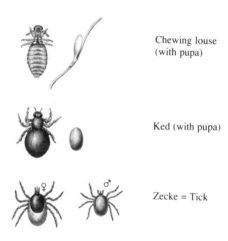

Chewing louse (with pupa)

Ked (with pupa)

Zecke = Tick

External parasites of sheep. Chewing lice commonly infest sheep and live on gland secretions, scales of skin, and bits of hair. Sucking lice suck blood. Ticks not only suck blood but can also carry pathogens.

Sucking lice also live on the skin of sheep, but they, like the much more common *chewing lice*, are quite a bit smaller than keds. *Ticks* also suck the sheep's blood and can be carriers of disease. Hard ticks of the Ixodidae family are widespread in many parts of the world. When ticks have sucked themselves full, they drop to the ground, where they reproduce. Sheep are also subject to *mites* that cause scabies or mange. The most serious of these ovine mites is *Psoroptes ovis.* Because of the economic losses mites can cause, the U.S. Department of Agriculture and state departments of agriculture have done extensive research and devised control measures, so that scabies is no longer a problem in the United States.

The easiest time to get rid of pests that spend their entire life cycle under the fleece is after shearing. In addition, the whole flock should be sprayed or dipped repeatedly after shearing. Ask your veterinarian what chemical he or she recommends. Single animals can be washed.

Harmful Insects

During the summer months, sheep are bothered by various insects, depending on the region.

Bot flies are dangerous because their larvae penetrate into the nasal passages and sinus cavities of the sheep. An infestation of nasal bot fly larvae requires the attention of a veterinarian to determine the best method of treatment.

Mosquitoes sometimes occur in great numbers near moving water and suck blood primarily from the sheeps' ears.

Blowflies of various species lay eggs in dirty skin folds, in festering sores, and on injured skin, where the eggs develop into maggots. There is no simple and lasting way to control these pests. One effort at prevention is to make sure all exposed skin is clean of manure and to avoid skin injuries or treat them promptly.

Internal Parasites
(Endoparasites)

Much more serious than the insects that prey on sheep from the outside are the various internal parasites—mostly worms—that live in their host's intestinal tract, liver, and lungs. Various kinds of *roundworms* are prevalent in sheep. These thin, threadlike worms lay masses of eggs in their host's intestines, which are then passed in the sheep's feces. The eggs or larvae of *lungworms,* large and

small *liver flukes,* and *tapeworms* (*Moniezia expansa*) and oocysts of *coccidia* are also found in the feces of sheep. These parasites in their first developmental stage (eggs, or oocysts) develop to their infectious stage (larvae) in the "outside world" of the pasture or the barn floor and are then picked up again by the sheep in food plants. To complete their life cycle the parasites need certain environmental conditions. Small lungworms, liver flukes, and tapeworms even need intermediary hosts (snails and mites). As a general rule one can say that warm temperatures, sufficient moisture in the ground, and a high stocking rate definitely encourage the spread of internal parasites. If sheep are kept off a pasture for a long period, many of the parasites eventually die, and the pasture again becomes usable for sheep.

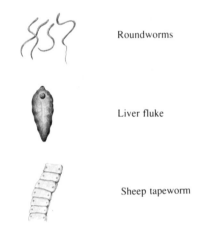

Roundworms

Liver fluke

Sheep tapeworm

Internal parasites of sheep. Internal parasites are much more harmful to sheep than external parasites. They produce masses of eggs that are excreted with the feces, develop on the ground, and are then ingested again by the sheep when they graze.

A microscopic examination of a sheep's feces, which can be done by a veterinarian or a veterinary laboratory, reveals the presence of endoparasites in abnormal numbers. It is useful to remember that parasites adapted to their hosts a long time ago when relatively few sheep roamed over large areas. A huge number of eggs had to be produced to ensure that a few larvae would be picked up by sheep that passed through the same places only infrequently. Domestic sheep, particularly if they are kept in great numbers on limited pastures or in paddocks, are forced to remain in a circumscribed area with accumulating amounts of manure. They have no way of getting away from the increasing masses of developing parasites. This is why some animals become infested with parasites, are weakened, and may succumb to them.

Worming

Today there are highly effective and safe medications that can be used in a planned schedule of treatment against almost all parasitic worms. However, for the reasons just mentioned, a permanent cure can be expected only if the animals are not continually re-exposed to the parasites. This is why wormings should coincide with a change of pasture. If at all possible, a pasture that has been grazed should next be cut for hay or silage. Alternating sheep with other grazing animals also reduces the danger of parasite infestation, since most intestinal parasites survive only in one host species. Worming should be done in the spring, before or shortly after lambing and before the sheep enter the new pasture. The sheep should be wormed again in the summer if analysis of their feces shows signs of infestation, and again late in the fall before they move indoors.

Hoof Problems

Foot rot is a widespread condition caused by bacteria. This chronic disease gradually destroys the horn of the affected hoof and also spreads to the inner hoof wall and the deeper layers of the hoof. Because of the pain caused by the disease, the animals limp badly and in extreme cases even crawl on their carpal joints. Foot rot is highly contagious

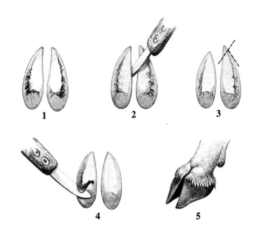

The hoofs of sheep must be trimmed and examined for changes and irregularities at least twice a year.
1 Hoof with edges rolled under; 2 Scraping out accumulated dirt; 3 Trimming the tips; 4 Cutting back the weight-bearing edges; 5 Hoof after corrective trimming.

to other animals that walk on the same ground. Hot and humid weather, muck, and manure further increase the likelihood of spreading the infection.

Treatment and Prevention: Hoofs affected by foot rot must be pared very carefully and any soft spots removed. The deep cuts inevitably start bleeding and must be treated with an appropriate drug, such as a chloramphenicol spray. Affected sheep should be separated from the rest of the flock and kept on clean, dry ground, and the parings must be carefully collected and destroyed (burned) to prevent further contamination.

To try to prevent hoof rot, the sheep's feet should be checked and the horn trimmed regularly, and the animals should be kept in a clean and dry area. You may even want to have them walk through disinfectant foot baths. Limping can also result from inadequate care (overgrown hoofs), or it can be a sign that hollow pockets have formed between the horny wall of the hoof and the inner hoof, where dirt accumulates. Sometimes sheep

If Your Sheep Get Sick

limp because there is a nail, a splinter, or thorn in the foot. In all these cases, relief can be provided only if the foreign object—if there is one—is removed and the problem spot that is causing inflammation is cut out by someone experienced in hoof care.

Diseases of the Digestive System

Sheep are ruminants and as such very sensitive to mistakes in feeding. Especially in the rumen—the first, largest, and most important division of the stomach—it is important that the pH value remain stable between 6.2 and 7 so that the digestion of plant cellulose can function with the aid of symbiotic bacteria and protozoas. The gas that is produced in this digestive process must rise up from the food pulp and be able to escape through periodic belching (see page 7).

Bloat (Tympanites): This sudden distension of the rumen occurs when the fermenting contents of the rumen become foamy. This happens primarily in the late spring and summer when sheep are more likely to overeat on fresh, lush food (especially clover and other legumes). This condition can quickly lead to death. Bloated sheep must be given bloat medicine immediately (a silicon preparation prescribed by the veterinarian). Sheep that are already lying on the ground and are unable to stand up should be killed. I don't recommend trying to puncture the rumen to relieve pressure because the procedure is rarely successful and can lead to peritonitis.

The best prevention is to give the sheep appropriate amount of aged, coarse food or hay before turning them loose on fresh young grass. Avoid rain- or dew-soaked pastures. Also make sure that they have plenty of drinking water available.

Ruminal Acidosis: If sheep gorge themselves on feed that is high in carbohydrates, especially if the feed was not introduced gradually enough for their system to adjust to it, the pH value in their rumens drops dramatically and leads to acidity of

the rumen. Sheep get very sick three to six hours after eating an excess of foodstuffs like grain, sugar beets, potatoes, or bread. The symptoms include inactivity of the rumen, highly accelerated breathing, apathy, and some bloating; death may follow. Sick animals must be given plenty of fresh water immediately and be treated by a veterinarian. This condition can be prevented if sheep are slowly introduced to the foodstuffs just mentioned. Never give them too much food like bread and sugar beets.

Ruminal Alkalosis: An abnormally low level of acidity is caused by the excessive formation of ammonia (NH^{3-}). The pH value rises to around 8 and becomes poisonous. The signs here are apathy, inactivity of the rumen, diarrhea, and liver damage. Alkalosis can result from the consumption of unclean and spoiled food (such as decomposing beet greens with too much dirt mixed in or improperly prepared silage). Under these conditions harmful foreign bacteria (of the genus *Proteus* and also *Escherichia coli*) multiply rapidly. Dangerous amounts of NH^{3-} can also form after overeating of feed concentrates high in protein (such as cracked soybeans). Sick animals must be given the highest quality hay, good carbohydrate feed, and clean drinking water immediately. Remove all the food that caused the problem.

Gastroenteritis: Diarrhea or scours is the most common sign of gastroenteritis, or intestinal inflammation, but repeated attempts to pass stool, loss of weight, and general ill health are also often seen. Lambs of various ages often come down with scours and are especially vulnerable to it. When diarrhea comes on and develops very quickly, it is usually caused by a combination of bacteria, viruses, or coccidia and feeding mistakes. Gradually developing and persistant diarrhea, on the other hand, is usually the result of worms. Bacterial diarrhea is especially frequent in young lambs. Coliform bacteria and the *Clostridium* species (anaerobic rod-shaped bacteria) are especially dangerous because they can cause the death not only of very young but also of nearly full-grown lambs. Lambs must be given prompt treatment at the first sign of diarrhea. If you are bottle-feeding lambs, take them off the milk immediately and give them clean water, tea, or an electrolyte solution. Diarrhea is treated with antibiotics, but prevention of dehydration is equally important.

Another important measure to combat scours is to house the affected animals in clean, dry quarters and give them good hay and fresh drinking water. If *Clostridium* infections (enterotoxemia) are a recurrent problem, you may want to build up resistance to the disease in your flock by vaccinating the ewes. An analysis of fecal samples can give you a good idea about how serious a problem coccidia and worms are. A different, chronic form of diarrhea that affects mostly older sheep and is incurable is called Johne's disease or paratuberculosis and requires different treatment.

Infectious Diseases

Sore mouth is a viral disease that affects primarily lambs and manifests itself in scabs on the lips and sometimes inside the mouth. It can be relatively harmless or quite serious. Topical application of antibiotics and general therapeutic measures help overcome it.

Foot-and-mouth disease is a viral infection that affects all cloven-footed animals. It takes a milder form in sheep than in cattle. The most frequent signs are lameness; the appearance of small blisters on the hoofs, nostrils, and possibly on the teats; excessive salivation; and temperatures up to 106°F (41°C). The disease subsides after a few days.

Some incurable viral infections affecting sheep are leukosis, rabies, scrapie, listeriosis, pulmonary adenomatosis, visna, and maedi (visna and maedi were first observed in Iceland and mean "wasting" and "breath" in Icelandic).

Leukosis can show up in a variety of ways and is typically chronic. Although the virus is quite common in sheep, the disease in its active stage,

manifested by anemia, edema, and swelling of the lymph nodes, is extremely rare.

Rabies attacks the nervous system and is spread by the bite of an infected animal (mostly foxes). The incubation stage can last from two weeks to three months. Sheep that have rabies often exhibit a hightened sexual drive (mounting), compulsive movements, salivating, and finally apathy. They become paralyzed and die after losing consciousness. The disease hardly ever spreads from one sheep to others.

Scrapie also attacks the central nervous system and sometimes has a lengthy incubation period of several months or even years. Its occurrence is usually restricted to certain geographic regions. This disease causes progressive loss of muscle control, which leads to strange behavior, including acting dazed, compulsive movements, and twisting or trotting motions.

Listeriosis (caused by bacteria) attacks the brain and is also characterized by strong behavioral symptoms such as compulsive movements, twisting and trotting without apparent cause, and a dazed demeanor.

Pulmonary adenomatosis and **maedi** are chronic lung ailments that affect mostly older sheep and result in increasingly poor condition, shortness of breath, lack of energy, and emaciation.

Regulations requiring prompt elimination of animals showing signs of these conditions are aimed at controlling and eradicating these diseases. Efforts to treat affected animals are doomed to failure and should therefore not be undertaken.

Tetanus infections are caused by the bacterium *Clostridium tetani*, which develops in wounds and produces toxins. Painful cramping of the skeletal muscles (distorted face and hunched posture) is the outward sign of the disease.

Sheep suffering from tetanus usually cannot be saved. Where tetanus is a problem, sheep should be vaccinated against the bacterium. Maintaining strictly sanitary conditions during lambing (disinfecting the navel) and during docking and castrating reduces the risk of infection.

If Your Sheep Get Sick

Deficiency Diseases

Lambs suffering from *white muscle disease* are weak, have trouble getting up, and usually die soon. A lack of selenium in the soil is the cause. The disease can be prevented if both ewes and lambs are given selenium and vitamin E supplements. Very occasionally a vitamin B deficiency can lead to an *infection of the brain* in lambs, especially in feeder lambs (lambs fattened for slaughter). Affected animals often display a curious "stargazing" stance.

Complications After Birth

Lambing time is a time of great physical demands and adjustments for the ewe that make her more susceptible to health problems. A strong, healthy ewe normally drops her lambs quickly and without complications, and the afterbirth is expelled soon after. The ewe is active, turns to her lambs, and soon resumes eating and drinking. Apathy, refusal to eat, and especially lying down (inability to get on her feet) are signs that require prompt attention, usually from a veterinarian.

Sometimes there are problems with the afterbirth. The afterbirth consists of fetal membranes and the placenta, a vascular organ that is connected to the uterine wall and supplies nourishment to the fetus. Sometimes some or all of the afterbirth fails to be released properly by the uterus, or part of it dangles from the vagina. Although sheep are generally quite immune to this complication of the birthing process, a consultation with the veterinarian and medication are in order. Occasionally the entire uterus is prolapsed and hangs from the vagina in a bloody cabbage-sized mass. The situation must be corrected as quickly as possible and the vaginal opening closed off.

During the first days after giving birth, injuries sustained during birthing or a problematic afterbirth can cause uterine infections, which can spread to other parts of the system if the animal is in a generally weakened state. Mastitis is also quite common, particularly in the early stages of nursing a lamb.

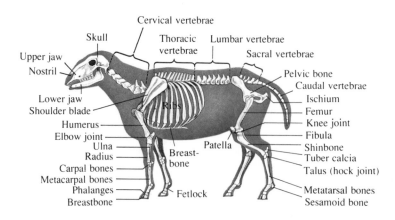

What is where on a sheep? Knowing the different parts of a sheep's skeleton is particularly useful when talking to the veterinarian.

If Your Sheep Get Sick

You can tell that a ewe has mastitis if her milk stops flowing and the affected part of the udder is swollen and feels hot and hard to the touch. Ewes often drag their hindlegs because of the pain caused by mastitis. Any infection must be treated promptly with the proper drugs to prevent further complications. In addition to infectious diseases, pregnant ewes are also subject to metabolic diseases, such as *milk fever* (*hypocalcemia*) and *ketosis* (*pregnancy toxemia*).

Someone with only a few sheep and limited experience should always seek the advice of a properly qualified person at the first sign of illness in his or her animals. Home remedies may occasionally help, such as massaging the udders with lard or feeding a sick sheep coffee, but for most serious infections and metabolic diseases they are useless and in fact harmful because they delay proper treatment.

Problems of New Lambs

Broken legs are quite common in newly born lambs. They are usually the result of becoming stuck somewhere or of being trampled by adult animals. Broken legs, especially in young lambs, should be set properly and provided with a stiff, cushioned support. Treated in this fashion, they usually heal completely and without complications. If you lack experience, you should let a veterinarian bandage the broken leg.

Lambs are also extremely vulnerable to *infections* during their first few days of life. Pathogens can enter through the mouth or the navel and cause *diarrhea, blood poisoning*, and *tetanus* (see pages 42–44). Coliform and clostridial infections as well as coccidiosis can cause the death of lambs during the first few days. Lambs with a vitamin E and selenium deficiency can succumb to *white muscle disease* (see page 44).

If you are a novice in the areas of sheep management and lamb raising, you should always consult a veterinarian at the first sign of illness.

This is how you give a sheep liquid medicine: Grip the lower jaw to hold the head steady, and raise it slightly; then insert a long syringe into the back of the mouth from the side.

The Most Important Diseases of Older Lambs

Enterotoxemia, caused by various kinds of *Clostridium* bacteria, accounts for serious losses in older lambs and young sheep. If these pathogens multiply rapidly in a lamb's intestines, the toxins released by the bacteria flood the organism and death can strike without warning, claiming animals, particularly well-nourished sheep, that have shown no previous signs of illness, such as diarrhea.

One form of enterotoxemia is sometimes called *pulpy kidney* because the kidneys of the victims show a pulpy or mushy consistency as revealed by autopsy. Apparently this disease is more likely to strike animals that are fed too well on food that is too rich (grain and bread). If deaths of this nature occur repeatedly in your flock, you should seriously consider vaccinating the ewes against this disease.

Coccidiosis can become a serious problem if animals live under crowded conditions on wet ground. Affected sheep suffer from diarrhea, become progressively weaker, and are more susceptible to bacterial infections. Oocysts of coccidia show up in examination of the stool samples under the microscope. The disease is treated with sulfa drugs. The best way to discourage reinfection is to keep the flock on dry ground, to clean out manure regularly, to keep feeding troughs clean, and to make sure the drinking water is always fresh.

Poisoning

If we disregard diseases caused by feeding mistakes that upset the functioning of the rumen, poisoning is quite rare in sheep.

Plant Poisons: Under normal conditions sheep hardly ever eat poisonous plants in dangerous amounts. Still, anyone who has sheep should know that quite a few common garden plants and ornamental shrubs are poisonous. Arbor vitae, yew, boxwood, spurge laurel, laburnum, and rhododendron are all harmful to sheep. Make sure that your sheep don't nibble on them, and don't mix cuttings of these plants in with the feed.

Copper Poisoning: Sheep are especially sensitive to high levels of copper in the food. The mineral supplements for cattle, for instance, contain too much copper for sheep. Commercial pig feed is especially dangerous. There have been cases of sheep coming down with copper poisoning after grazing on meadows fertilized with pig manure.

Sodium Chloride Poisoning: If sheep have been deprived of salt for some time and then have unlimited access to it, they may ingest too much too quickly, and if not enough drinking water is available, fatal poisoning may follow. The daily requirement of salt (NaCl) for sheep is about $\frac{1}{5}$ ounce (5 g);

a dose of about 7 ounces (200 g) can be deadly.

Poisoning from Herbicides and Chemical Fertilizers: Modern agriculture relies heavily on herbicides, and pastures bordering on cultivated fields often receive a share of the spray if the wind is from the wrong direction. Especially in the spring, the time of most concentrated application of chemicals, you should not give your sheep feed that has been recently exposed to spraying.

Pastures that have been treated with chemical fertilizers should not be used by sheep until rain has washed the fertilizer into the soil and it has been completely absorbed by the soil.

Poisoning Caused by Feed: Grain or hay that is contaminated with certain molds can cause poisoning in sheep, and you should consequently never give your animals anything that is visibly moldy.

A Medicine Cabinet for Sheep

Anyone who keeps sheep should have some items on hand for treating minor problems. Among the basics are:

• Clippers or shears, a thermometer, and a syringe (for giving worm medication orally)
• A disinfectant or antibiotic spray (for treating minor wounds and the umbilical cord of newborn lambs as well as for minor hoof problems)
• An antibloat medication that can be given to the animals at the first sign of bloat

People the world over make their living keeping sheep. Above, left: A Portuguese shepherd milking; above, right, and below: Anatolian peasant women working with sheep's wool.
On the next page: Shearing sheep

The Products of Sheep

Wool

Wool is one of the oldest textile fibers, and the use of wool is still on the increase. Australia has the largest number of sheep, and most of the world's wool comes from that country. New Zealand, the Soviet Union, and the United States are also major producers of wool. Of about 6 billion pounds of raw wool that are produced worldwide annually, the United States accounts for about 110 million pounds.

Different Kinds of Wool

The main suppliers of the finest wool—merino wool—are South Africa and Australia. Merino sheep have hair that is up to 4 inches (10 cm) long, fine, and wavy and lends itself perfectly to manufacture into wool.

Coarse wool comes from many breeds that originated in England and Scotland and from regional breeds. The hair of these sheep is longer—anywhere from to 5 to 12 inches (12–30 cm)—coarse and strong and has less crimp than that of merinos. The wool made from the fleeces of these sheep is less soft than merino wool but stands up better to wear.

There is also "crossbred" wool, which comes from sheep that are crosses between merinos and English breeds. This wool is especially good for textiles that must be strong. Here, too, there are finer and coarser varieties.

Qualities of Sheep's Hair and of Wool

The hairs of a sheep's coat don't stand up separately but cling together in locks. The wool of the entire coat in one piece is called a fleece. One sheep produces about 4 to 8 pounds (2–4 kg) of pure, washed wool annually. The best wool comes from sheep up to seven years old. After that, the wool loses some of its luster and pliancy. Sheep wool is coated with fat to keep out rain and cold. The fat helps to hold the fleece together so that it forms a warm, water-repellent coat.

You may be able to sell your fleeces to a wool pool or a local mill. In the United States there is a wool incentive program through which people who sell raw wool may receive payments based on the national average price paid for wool. Your county agricultural extension agent can inform you about the current status of the program. In the course of processing raw wool, such impurities as sweat, dirt, and suint (the natural waxes and grease found in sheep's wool) are removed. The suint is purified and made into lanolin. If you have only a few sheep you may prefer processing the wool yourself. There are many ways of turning wool into articles of clothing or other textiles, and if you knit or weave, you have a chance to enjoy the wonderful qualities of sheep's wool.

Sheep's hairs are not solid all the way through; instead each hair is made up of several layers with air trapped between them. This explains the remarkable insulating quality of woolen materials.

Wool is made up of protein molecules that resemble those of human skin, and because of the similarity in the two substances, the human body usually feels comfortable in woolen clothing. Wool is soft and elastic. If it is stretched, it eventually contracts back to its original length. The crimp of sheep's hair accounts for this elasticity, as well as for the insulating quality of wool and its ability to absorb moisture. Woolen clothes can rapidly absorb as much as 35% of their weight in moisture without feeling wet. This moisture can come from the outside in the form of rain or from inside, as sweat. This is why woolen sweaters are said to keep you from catching cold and why fishermen like to wear them (Icelandic sweaters).

Heat, friction, and weak alkaline solutions can cause individual wool fibers to mat together into felt. In this felted form, wool is manufactured into cloth, carpets, and upholstery textiles that are solid, dense, and impermeable to heat and water. Felted wool is excellent for making into outer garments, such as jackets and coats, and into blankets. Felting is not desirable in knitted garments, however, because it destroys the very qualities we like in sweaters and other knitted items, namely, their softness and their ability to fit different contours. This is why woolen garments should never be rubbed and wrung when being washed, nor spun dried in a washing machine. Woolen clothing should always be washed and dried at low temperatures. Drying it in the sun or near a stove may cause felting.

Woolen textiles of high quality have a soft sheen to them, particularly if they are made from merino wool. Wool may also be pressed into permanent shapes if heat and moisture are applied. This is how trousers acquire permanent creases and skirts are pleated.

You are undoubtedly aware that synthetic materials tend to accumulate electric charges that can cause crackling sounds and sometimes even sparks that are visible in the dark. An accumulation of electric static can cause headaches and symptoms of fatigue. There are no such reactions to woolen clothing because it does not build up electric charges.

Raw Sheep Wool

Shearing: Sheep must be kept under very clean conditions so that the fleece does not become contaminated with dirt and plant material. If the animals are clipped only once a year, the wool fibers are longer and easier to work with. A proper shearing job produces a fleece in one piece (see color photo on page 56).

Sorting: Wool is sorted immediately after shearing. The fleece of a sheep is not all of the same quality. The quality of fleeces varies from sheep to sheep, depending on the animal's age, sex, and breed, as well as on what it has been eating and how it is being kept.

The finest wools are used for making felt, knitting, and weaving. The coarse wools are used for ordinary pillow and mattress stuffing.

Washing: If your sheep have been kept very clean, repeated gentle washing of the fleece in warm rainwater suffices. Usually there is not much dirt in the fleece, and whatever dirt there is can be removed simply by washing the wool in mild soap and then rinsing it well with clear water.

Not all the wool of a fleece is of the same quality: 1 indicates the best, 6 the poorest wool.

To keep the wool beautiful during washing and to prevent felting:

• Use the recommended amount of soap.
• Squeeze the water out of the wool without wringing or rubbing.
• Use water of an even temperature (about 98° F, 37° C) for both washing and rinsing.

Do not wash the wool in a washing machine.

If you place the wool in bags with a loose weave, you can wash and rinse it in convenient small batches. Dry it on a rack or screen, preferably in the shade because direct sun, as well as the heat from a stove, can have a deleterious effect.

Storing: Wool may absorb a great deal of moisture and should therefore be packed in burlap bags and kept in an airy, dry attic. Unwashed wool is relatively safe from moths because moths don't like the sweat in the wool. Washed wool should be packed in paper bags or bags of tightly woven cotton. Take precautions against moths!

Processing Wool

Carding: Use only clean wool for carding. In carding, the wool fibers are disentangled and brushed and combed to make them lie parallel in strands that can be spun. Learning to card is not very difficult. Carding tools come in different sizes and designs. The smaller hand tools are slow and make sense only for small amounts of wool. The larger tools are expensive, and the cost is justified only if you plan to process a lot of wool. Almost any woolen mill will card wool for you if you pay for the service. Find out what you would have to pay and calculate whether investing in a carding machine still makes sense. Don't forget to count the hours of your labor.

Spinning: Combed wool works best for spinning. You can use either a distaff and spindle or a spinning wheel. Spindle and distaff are cheaper, but a spinning wheel is more efficient for spinning significant amounts of wool. Spinning is easiest to learn by observation and practice, and the best way is to be able to watch an experienced spinner. You can also learn spinning in courses offered in community education programs, and in Europe there are hobby vacation packages that include spinning instruction. Foot-treadle spinning wheels work very well for spinning at home.

Twining Wool into Knitting Yarn: Because they are twisted tightly, the single-ply yarns produced with the spindle or spinning wheel would result in a twisted piece of work if they were knitted as they are. Single-ply yarns also tear too easily. If you take two strands twisted in the same direction and twine them together in the opposite direction, however, the strands unwind somewhat, and the resulting two-ply yarn is quite strong. If you take three strands, you end up with three-ply yarn. You can also mix colors to get different effects. Yarn made up of two plies, one from the wool of a black sheep and the other from wool of a white sheep, is called "salt-and-pepper."

Once the yarn is spun, it is wound in skeins, washed, and hung from a bar in the shade to dry. It now retains its shape and is ready to be used.

Uses of Wool

Knitting and Crocheting: These crafts have in recent years become popular again, and many people are now knitting or crocheting as a hobby. If you use hand-spun yarn, you should be very choosy about what you make out of it. Find a traditional old pattern or, better yet, design your own.

You can also use unspun wool for knitting or crocheting if you use it along with a thin woolen yarn. Take about 12 to 16 inches (30–40 cm) of the fleece into your left hand, along with the woolen yarn. Run the yarn through the fleece. The fleece adheres to the yarn, which you can build up this way to any desired thickness. Be very careful to keep this newly formed strand even. You can now knit this yarn into simple patterns. Don't pull out more than about 20 inches (50 cm) at a time, or the strand will pull apart since the fibers are merely pressed loosely together, not twisted the way they are in spun wool. Garments made this way are especially warm because the unspun fibers loosely fill the loops of the stitches. In time the fibers interlock and add more stability to the weave.

The different qualities of spun and unspun wool and their different colors lend an additional visual effect to whatever knitting pattern you use. Since the lanolin has not been removed, your garment is even water repellent.

You cannot unravel a piece of knitting that incorporates unspun wool. This is why you should definitely first knit a sample piece to make sure your finished item is the right size. For the sample, knit a square piece, and then count how many stitches and rows make up 4 inches (10 cm). It is then easy to figure out how many stitches to cast on for your pattern.

Weaving: I first became aware of weaving as a hobby when a Stockholm friend of mine made me a present of a hand-woven red-and-white belt. Belts, ribbons, and scarves can be made easily and with practically no instruction on small, simple hand looms that you can buy at most craft shops. If you are thinking of working with a regular shuttle loom, however, you should first take a course in weaving. Such courses are sometimes offered in adult education programs. In Europe, travel agents also offer hobby vacation packages that include

The Products of Sheep

weaving or spinning classes. These plans are gaining increasing popularity. Most instruction manuals on weaving include a section on how to build simple looms. If you are thinking of becoming a professional weaver, however, you should enroll in a school that has a program in this craft.

Making Felt: The natural felting property of hair is especially strong in the fine, crimped fibers of sheep's wool. Overlapping cuticular scales make the hairs of sheep feel rough when rubbed from the tip to the root but almost smooth when rubbed the other way. Pounding the fibers presses them together and causes the scales to interlock so tightly that they can no longer spring back into their original shape despite their natural elasticity. This irreversible entanglement of the fibers is called the directional frictional effect. In the spaces between the fibers, air is trapped, which is why felt is a warm and insulating material. In the industrial manufacture of fine, tight felt fabrics, various mechanical and chemical processes are used. If you make felt at home, you must rely primarily on physical exertion. Heat and alkaline solutions also help turn wool into felt. Start by placing as many thin layers of carded wool as possible one on top of the other. If you like, you can arrange them in abstract or figurative patterns. When you have assembled the whole piece, lay it on a thin cloth, roll it up in the cloth, pour boiling, soapy water (soft soap) over it, and then start kneading and squeezing. Watch out for folds or wrinkles. These must be smoothed out immediately because they will not come out later and will ruin your pattern. Felting is an undesirable property in wool that is woven or knitted by hand or machine because it destroys the elasticity of the fabric and results in shapeless garments (see page 50).

Milk and Milk Products

The Qualities of Fresh Milk

Sheep's milk compares well with the milk of any of our other domestic milking animals. It tastes delicious, and its high nutritional value is undisputed. Many people ascribe to it almost mystical medicinal and life-prolonging qualities. Cows and even goats may yield larger quantities, but sheep's milk is much richer in essential nutrients.

The water content of cow's milk and goat's milk is about 88%; in sheep's milk it is only about 83.5%. Sheep's milk also contains about one-third more protein, fat, and milk sugar than cow's milk, and some vitamins are present in it in much higher concentrations. Some of these are vitamin B13 and vitamin B17; the latter is said to aid cell regeneration and inhibit cancer. However, the assertion one hears now and then that sheep never contract cancer is untrue.

Sheep have smaller teats than cows or goats, so that you can use only a couple of fingers, not the whole hand, when milking.

Milking Sheep

The teats of sheep are much smaller than those of cows and goats. This makes milking them harder because you can use only a couple of fingers rather than the entire hand (see color photo on page 55). There is no point in describing in detail how to milk a sheep because it is a skill that must be acquired through practice. Try to find an owner of milking sheep who will show you how to do it. Milking machines for sheep have been developed, but buying one is worthwhile only if you have enough animals for a commercial dairy operation.

The key to milking sheep well and without hurting the animals is that they be tame. It takes a lot of patience and soothing talk to convince a ewe to let herself be milked without putting up a struggle or attempting to bolt. Giving her some grain to eat while you milk her often helps. Proper preparation of the udder before you start milking is also important. Massaging the udder stimulates the production of the hormone oxytocin, which causes milk to flow from the udder into the teats. If the ewe still holds her milk back, jabbing the udder with your hand may do the trick (lambs often butt when nursing to stimulate milk flow). To prevent mastitis from developing and to get the last, fattiest milk, you must milk the animal thouroughly and gently. You should always milk into a clean bucket. Since you cannot avoid bits of hay and wool as well as insects dropping into the milk, you should strain it immediately after milking. Pour it into a clean container through a milk strainer with a washable stainless steel filter or a disposable cloth filter. If necessary, a clean linen cloth will do. Then store the milk immediately in a refrigerator.

Uses of Fresh Milk

Fresh sheep's milk is most nutritious if it is kept refrigerated and is drunk soon after milking, when it still has all the nutrients and vitamins, some of which are lost in processing. If you freeze individual portions of milk, you can have fresh milk even when all your ewes have gone dry (toward the end of pregnancy) and before they freshen again. Fresh milk should not be kept in a freezer longer than about six months, however. You can thaw the milk by placing the container in lukewarm water, but make sure the milk does not become too warm.

Fresh sheep's milk is also excellent in milkshakes with various kinds of fruit. If taken in coffee or tea, it is comparable to evaporated milk. Of course you can also use sheep's milk for cooking and baking, but it is better to dilute it somewhat with water to keep it from curdling when heating it. There is no need to scald sheep's milk before drinking it because tuberculosis is practically unknown among sheep and you can tell when milking if a ewe is suffering from mastitis caused by bacterial infection.

Sour Milk, Pot Cheese, and Yoghurt

If you let fresh milk stand long enough it turns sour by itself. Various bacteria and fungi convert the milk sugar (lactose) into lactic acid as they multiply. The warmer the temperature, the faster the process takes place.

Unlike cow's milk, sheep's milk hardly gets thick when souring; you must add rennet (available at drugstores). If you pace the sour milk curd in a cloth, letting the whey run off, you end up with a pot cheese that you can use like regular cottage cheese. Whey contains valuable protein and should not be thrown out. It can be used as a drink, fed to animals, or used in skin care (washing with whey).

If you want to make yoghurt, the milk must be kept at an even 105 to 110° F (40–43° C) after certain bacterial cultures have been added to it (natural food stores carry yoghurt cultures). You can also mix some commercial live-culture yoghurt into the milk instead of buying a culture. Making yoghurt is easiest with an electric yoghurt maker. After keeping the milk and yoghurt mixture warm for about eight to twelve hours, place it in the refrigerator, and the yoghurt will be ready to eat the next day. A half-pint container of unflavored commercial live-culture yoghurt is enough to make six glasses of homemade yoghurt. Use one glassful to mix with milk for the next batch of yoghurt to keep the process going.

Making Butter

Butter is made from milk fat. It takes about 8 quarts of milk to make a pound of butter. To make butter, the cream must be separated from the milk. This is done most easily with a centrifuge, but you can also skim the cream off the top of the milk with a spoon and collect it for several days, keeping it in the refrigerator. Then, if you "churn" the accumulated cream by beating it in a blender or whipping it with an egg beater, you end up with clumps of butter. Let the whey drain from the clumps of butter in a sieve, and wash and knead the butter until the rinse water is clear. The resulting clean, white butter is often lightly salted (about ⅙ ounce or 5g of salt per pound of butter) to keep it fresh longer and to flavor it. Butter can be pressed in wooden or metal butter molds with attractive patterns. Warm the outside of the mold lightly to help the block of butter slide out. Butter can also be stored in small ceramic pots.

Making Cheese

Originally the main reason for making cheese was to turn periodic milk surpluses into a product that would keep. The basic principle of cheesemaking is to let the protein (casein) coagulate into curds and to remove some of the water. You can start either with sweet milk, to which you add rennet, or with sour milk. Cheeses that contain a relatively high percentage of water are called soft cheeses. Hard cheeses have more of the water removed. Different varieties of cheese are obtained through the action of various microorganisms and through different degrees of ripening. Making your own cheese requires experience. Experiment with small quantities, and don't be discouraged if your first attempts fail to live up to the ideals of your imagination. Temperature is an important factor in cheesemaking. You should have a cheese thermometer to make sure that you are working at precisely the right temperatures. Most cheeses take a long time to ripen and must be stored for weeks in rooms kept at certain temperatures, and the cheeses must be turned periodically. If you decide to become a hobby cheesemaker, you should consult books on the subject (see Literature and Addresses, page 60).

There is a simple recipe for homemade sheep cheese that I would like to share here. Heat 7 quarts (7 liters) of sheep's milk to exactly 77° F (25° C) (check with a cooking thermometer). Then add 7 or 8 drops of rennet, and heat slowly to 95° F (35° C). It should take about forty minutes for the curd to form. Put the pot in a cool place (room temperature is cool enough), and stir briefly when the milk begins to coagulate. Afterward the whey is drained off by putting the coagulated milk into a sieve lined with cheesecloth. Take the cheese with cheesecloth out after about an hour, and place it in a cheese mold. Cheese molds are available commercially, or you can make your own. If you want to make small cheeses (for which you use smaller pieces of cheesecloth), square or round plastic dishes (such as margarine containers) can be used. Simply punch plenty of holes in the bottom and sides with a nail. Then place the cheese, wrapped in its cloth, in the dish, cover it with a plate of the right size, weigh down the plate with rocks, and let the cheese sit for an hour. Then you take it out, remove the cheesecloth, and return it to the dish, weighing it down again with plate and rocks. This time you leave it for 24 hours. When you take it out now, it holds its shape. Place it in a salt bath (about 4 ounces, 100 g, of salt per quart of water) so that it is submerged. It should stay in the bath for about 24 hours and be turned several times. Then you take the cheese out and let it dry uncovered for about three days in a well-ventilated spot, somewhere, obviously, where no flies, mice, or cats can get at it.

Washing the cheese with saltwater helps prevent premature ripening (formation of mold).

Rennet will keep for months in a refrigerator.

Meat

Some Thoughts on the Subject of Killing Animals for Food

One of the basic facts of life on this earth is that new creatures are born all the time and that others

The Products of Sheep

die. All of them—some more obviously than others—depend for their nourishment on other creatures that either are killed or have died a natural death. The human is not by nature vegetarian. Prehistoric evidence, as well as the existence of certain parasites, makes that clear. If we accept as natural that people eat meat, then we also have to accept the keeping and slaughtering of domestic animals.

Modern methods of mass production, however, impose on the majority of domestic animals conditions that seem appalling to people who are attuned to nature and regard even cows and chickens as creatures that have highly developed senses and certain basic requirements.

Be assured, however, that qualified persons have now developed techniques of killing an animal that are painless and cause no panic. (In contrast to human beings, animals cannot imagine death.) You then have a right to enjoy the meat without feelings of guilt.

All animals for slaughter are subject to inspection before and after slaughtering. After receiving the inspector's approval, the meat may be used at home or sold. For more information, consult your state extension specialist.

The cleanly skinned and gutted carcass may be hung in a suitable place for several days in cool weather. In some areas, locker space may be rented. While it is hanging, the meat undergoes a natural chemical processes (curing) that makes it more tender and flavorful.

Cutting up the halves of a sheep carcass is not very difficult for an experienced meat cutter. First, shanks are cut following the curve of the ribs. Then the flanks are trimmed and the ends of the ribs are sawn off, leaving enough rib attached to the backbone to form chops. The legs, along with the attached pelvic sections, are removed. The remaining parts of the neck, back, and breast can be cut into stewing meat.

The legs and the rack make the best roasts, and the ribs, breast, and brisket of young lamb are very tasty if grilled, braised, or stewed.

Different Kinds of Lamb

Lambs up to about six months are sold as *spring lambs*. They are usually butchered when they are three to six months old. The meat of spring lamb is tender and light-colored and tastes milder than older lamb. Spring lamb is considered a delicacy and fetches a high price.

Meat sold as *lamb* is from animals older than spring lambs, up to one year old. The meat is somewhat denser than spring lamb and a deep pink. It is comparable in quality to spring lamb and can be cooked in similar ways.

Yearling lamb comes from sheep that are one to two years old. It, too, makes good roasts, although it is even denser than lamb and has a stronger flavor.

The meat from sheep up to four years old is called *mutton*. It is very tasty but has a characteristic mutton flavor and is deep red.

Both lamb and mutton are used primarily for roasting. The loin and legs make the best roasts. Lamb chops—and steaks cut from the leg—are also very tender if the meat has been cured properly. Neck, breast, and flank meat is best used as stew meat. Because of its strong smell and taste the meat from older animals (old ewes and rams) is not very popular with most people, but some Near-Eastern ethnic groups like it.

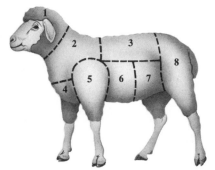

Side view of a sheep showing where the most important cuts of lamb come from.
1 head; 2 neck; 3 back and loin; 4 brisket; 5 shoulder and shank; 6 ribs; 7 flank; 8 leg of lamb

The Products of Sheep

If you have an old ewe or ram that is no longer of any use but that you are reluctant to see it go to an uncertain fate by selling it, you should consider having the animal slaughtered for you. If you trim out the fat and run the meat through a meat grinder it makes good ground meat, which you can use for sausage or freeze in small packages and later use for mutton patties, meatloaf, and so on.

Meat that might be tough can be tenderized by being hung longer after butchering, or it can be cooked in a pressure cooker or a microwave oven until it is soft and tender.

The Black Sheep Newsletter Cookbook includes a wide variety of ideas on how lamb can be prepared. Good recipes can also be found in *Good Old Food* and *Eating Meat and Staying Healthy* (see the bibliography on page 60).

Making Sausage

The meat of older sheep, including that of old rams, can be utilized for sausage. It makes sense even for a small household to turn a whole animal into sausage. You can also save some of the best cuts for roasts or a leg for smoking like a ham.

Before you embark on making sausage, you must buy a few items from a butcher. You need raw, that is, unsalted and unsmoked pork fat and sausage casings. It is best to order these ahead so that the butcher will have them ready for you. Natural sausage casings are heavily salted and therefore must be soaked in water for 24 hours and then rinsed several times very thoroughly both inside and out. Be careful not to puncture or tear the casings in the process.

You also need a sausage stuffer to use with your meat grinder. This attachment is not very expensive, and you should buy one if you like homemade sausage.

Trimming the raw meat off the bones is a time-consuming job. The meat is then put through the meat grinder. If you decide to buy an electric grinder, you should get a good, solid machine like those used in small butcher shops. An ordinary household meat grinder is adequate for making a portion of beef tartar now and then, but it is not up to chopping up an entire sheep. Use the fine or the medium blade, and run the meat through a second time when you stuff it into the casings.

Insert about 3 feet (1 m) of casing into the sausage stuffer when you start. The stuffing is best done by two persons, with one of them putting the meat into the grinder and running the machine and the other holding the stuffed sausage and tying it off when it reaches the desired length. You can use casing or cotton string for tying the ends of the sausages.

Proper seasoning is the secret of making good sausage. Many home butchers use only salt, pepper, and marjoram in various proportions. Some people also recommend coriander, but be cautious with the amounts, so that one seasoning does not predominate above the others.

If you can sausage, follow the usual rules for canning: use clean jars and new lids, and observe the recommended cooking temperatures and times exactly.

The seasoned sausage meat is filled into jars or cans—not too full—and the tops are screwed on. Place the jars or cans in a canner, heat to 212° F (100° C), and boil for two hours. After two days, heat again to the same temperature for one hour. The jars should always cool slowly. Label the jars, and store them in a cool, dark place.

Sheep Manure

Sheep manure, especially compost made with a lot of sheep manure, is one of the best fertilizers for gardens as well as for fields and pastures.

The Behavior of Sheep

From the time when humans first started to domesticate sheep, an understanding of the animals' behavior has been not only very useful but indeed necessary for the animals to thrive under conditions of domestication. People close to nature have probably always interpreted animal behavior intuitively and based their treatment of animals on this intuitive knowledge. Only in fairly recent times has the behavior of animals become the subject of systematic study. This field of study is called *ethology*. This new science has greatly increased our general knowledge of animal behavior and has laid to rest many views that falsely attributed human feelings and motives to animals. Comparative studies of different species—and comparisons with humans—have revealed many basic similarities as well as significant differences between species. Familiarity with the typical behavior of a given species and awareness of the basic needs of specific domestic animals are prerequisites for any meaningful programs of animal protection and for the proper treatment of pets as well as livestock. Each kind of animal has its own inborn behavior, instincts, and reflexes, but through imprinting and through the repetition of experience some behavior patterns can be modified and the animals better adapted to the particular environment in which they live.

The Herd Instinct

Sheep are herbivorous ruminants, and like many other ungulates, they live in herds or flocks. Herds tend to stay in the same area. The herd instinct is very strongly developed in sheep. If a few animals begin bolting in flight, all the others inevitably follow, regardless of obstacles and dangers (such as a dangerous precipice). It is almost impossible to divert part of the flock and lure them in a different direction or to separate individual sheep from a running flock. Lambs that were bottle-fed and raised in close contact with humans tend to view

these humans as belonging to the flock as well. When sheep sense danger, are frightened, and resort to flight, the herd crowds together more and more tightly. This is why sheep can be herded with dogs.

Food Intake

Sheep spend most of the day (eight to twelve hours) eating. They graze longest and most actively early in the morning and again in the late afternoon, always moving in a forward direction. Periods of grazing are followed by periods of resting and ruminating. Chewing the cud takes about eight to ten hours a day and is done in eight to fifteen sessions. Sheep nibble off plants close to the ground, preferring some over others, and choosing them according to smell and taste. They avoid plants and areas that are contaminated with sheep dung. This "repugnance" for excreta of their own species is characteristic of grazing animals in general and probably emerged in the course of evolution because most parasites of the alimentary canal are transmitted in an immature form in the host's feces.

Sheep apparently defecate wherever they happen to be (about eight to ten times a day) and thus distribute their manure fairly evenly over the entire pasture.

Battles of Rivalry and Behavoir During Heat

Most European sheep breeds experience estrus in the fall. At this time a certain restlessness enters the flock. Rams, especially, are likely to engage in contests, charging at each other from some distance with lowered heads. Generally these battles result in no serious injuries, although I once witnessed a strong, fully grown, black-faced ram dropping to the ground as though hit by lightning after one of these head-on collisions. Very tame rams sometimes also charge at people. This can be a serious matter, especially if the attack takes you by surprise. To try to prevent the butting habit scratch the ram only on the throat, never on the head.

The Bond Between Mother and Child

It is impressive how quickly the bond between mother and child is established in sheep after birth. The ewe immediately turns to her newborn lamb and licks it vigorously, and within a couple of hours the lamb has found its mother's udder and is drinking the colostrum. Ewes first recognize their lambs by the smell; later they can also tell them apart from other lambs by their looks and voices. A ewe will push other lambs away and not let them nurse. Sometimes, especially in the older breeds, a ewe that has given birth to twins accepts only one of the lambs and rejects the other.

During the first few days, lambs nurse about sixteen times a day for about two minutes. Later the ewe often starts butting them away after only ten or twenty seconds of nursing. While the lambs are sucking, they wiggle their tails furiously. Presumably they do this to stimulate the ewe to check and sniff their rear ends. As the lambs grow older, the closeness between mother and offspring diminishes, and after a few months almost disappears.

Play Behavior

Almost everybody has probably at some point or other been enchanted by the exuberant gamboling of lambs on a sunny spring day. The high leaps with all four feet leaving the ground at once and the energetic racing around are a sign of the tremendous need for movement these young creatures have. In anticipation of skills that will be required later in life, the play of lambs is made up primarily of

elements simulating flight, battles of rivalry, and sexual behavior. Some of the play behavior also seems to arise from curiosity and an active interest in exploring the world.

An Unusual Behavioral Trait

If you place sheep in a position that is alien to them (setting them up on their haunches to trim their hoofs, for instance) or if they happen to find themselves lying on their backs, the animals usually remain motionless in that position for a long time, without making any effort to get back on their feet. Sometimes shy animals, when they find themselves captured, drop to the ground and remain there no matter what you do to them, refusing to get up and walk. One summer evening some alarmed strangers came to my door, reporting with great agitation that a dead ewe had been lying in her paddock for some time and that the orphaned lambs were running around bleating pitifully. When I rushed to the scene, I was indeed met with a sad picture. As soon as I helped the "dead" mother sheep back on her feet, however, she cheerfully trotted over to her lambs. Apparently she had been resting in the sun on a slope and had inadvertently slid into a half-reclining position from which she was unable to right herself, probably because of her thick coat. After a while she stopped trying to get up and just lay there, apparently resigned to her fate. The inability to get up again after rolling on the back can occur with increased frequency during late pregnancy and may, with insufficient supervision, lead to death by suffocation.

Social Behavior

One of the remarkable facts about sheep is that all the members of a flock always do the same thing at the same time without any one of them seeming to take on a "leadership position." Unlike goats, sheep get along with each other very peacefully.

The sheep in a flock maintain contact among themselves by bleating, with ewes and their lambs bleating most loudly and anxiously when they are separated. Single sheep always seek contact with other sheep or with a flock. Because of this great need for contact with other sheep—occasionally another kind of creature is accepted as a substitute—and because single sheep are extremely nervous and fearful, you should always keep at least two sheep together.

Literature and Addresses

Publications

Black Sheep Newsletter
1690 Butler Creek Road
Ashland, Oregon 97520
(Newsletter for small flock and colored sheep raisers; also publishes good lamb cookbook.)

"SHEEP!!!" Magazine
Box 32
Jefferson, Wisconsin 53549
(Best sheep publication for small flocks.)

"Shepherd" Magazine
5696 Johnson Road
New Washington, Ohio 44854
(Sheep magazine for small flocks.)

Spin-Off
Interweave Press
306 N. Washington Avenue
Loveland, Colorado 80537
(Specialty magazine for those interested in handspinning.)

Books

Black sheep Newsletter Cookbook.
Black sheep Newsletter, Ashland, Oregon

Chalmers, Irena Good Old Food. Barron's Educational Series, Inc., Hauppauge, New York.

Downing, Elizabeth *Keeping Sheep.* Pelham Books, London.

Levy, Josephine Bacon *Eating Meat and Staying Healthy.* Barron's Educational Series, Inc. Hauppauge, New York.

Midwest Plan Service, *Sheep Handbook of Housing and Equipment.* Iowa State University, Ames, Iowa

Parker, Ronald B. *The Sheep Book: A Handbook for the Modern Shepherd.* Scribner, New York.

Pointing, Kenneth *Sheep of the World in Colour.* Blanford, Dorset.

Simmons, Paula *Raising sheep the Modern Way.* Garden Way, Charlotte, Vermont

——— *Spinning and Weaving with Wool.* Pacific Search, Seattle, Washington.

——— *Turning Wool Into a Cottage Industry.* Madrona, Austin, Texas.

Spinning and Weaving (bibliography). The Unicorn, Petaluma, California

Literature and Addresses

Useful Addresses

National Sheep Association
Jenkins Lane
Tring, Herts
Great Britain
(Publishes a quarterly magazine, *The Sheep Farmer*)

National Wool Growers Association
1301 Pennsylvania Avenue, N.W.
Room 300
Washington, DC 20004
(Sponsers research in sheep diseases and other industry problems.)

Sheep Industry Development Program, Inc. (SID)
200 Clayton Street
Denver, Colorado 80206
(Gathers, evaluates, and disseminates research information on sheep production and management; publishes the *SID Research Digest.*)

Alden Amos
P.O. Box 196
Volcano, California 95689
(Charkas, spindles, wool combs, spinning wheels.)

Louet Sales Co.
P.O. Box 70
Carleton Place, Ontario, Canada K7C 3Pe
(Inexpensive and popular spinning wheel.)

Patrick Green Carders Ltd.
48793 Chilliwack Lake Road
Sardis, B.C., Canada V2R 2P1
(Wool carders and wool pickers; books)

Sheepman Supply Co.
P.O. Box 100
Barbroursville, Virginia 22923
(Catalog for $.50; sheepraising supplies.)

Index

Numbers in *italics* indicate color photographs

Index

Perfect for Pet Owners!

Ferrets
Chuck and Fox Morton
A Complete Pet Owner's Manual

Longhaired Cats
Grace Pond

Snakes
Klaus Griehl
Giant Snakes

Hans-J. Ullmann
The New Dog Handbook
Choosing a Dog • Training • Care & Feeding • Health • Understanding Dogs

PET OW...

Over 50 ill...
more colo...

AFRICAN...
AMAZON...
BANTAMS...
BEAGLES...
BEEKEEPI...
BOXERS (...
CANARIE...
CATS (242...
CHINCHIL...
CHOW-CH...
COCKATIE...
DACHSHU...
DOBERMA...
DWARF RA...
FANCY PIG...
FEEDING A...
    EUROPE...
FERRETS (...
GERBILS (...
GERMAN S...
GOLDEN R...
GOLDFISH...
GUINEA PIG...
HAMSTERS...
LABRADOR...
LIZARDS IN...
    (3925-4)
LONG-HAIR...
LOVEBIRDS...
MICE (2921...
MUTTS (412...
MYNAS (36...
NONVENOM...OUS SNAKES (5632-9)
PARAKEETS (2423-0)
PARROTS (2630-6)
PONIES (2856-2)
POODLES (2812-0)
RABBITS (2615-2)

...CAT FANCIER'S SERIES
Authoritative, colorful guides (over
35 color photos), 72 pp., paperback.
BURMESE CATS (2925-9)
LONGHAIR CATS (2923-3)
SIAMESE CATS (2924-0)

...MIUM SERIES
...prehensive, lavishly illustrated
...nces (60-300 color photos),
...76 pp., hardcover.
...ARIUM FISH SURVIVAL
...NUAL (5686-8)
...CARE MANUAL (5765-1)
...PLETE BOOK OF
...DGERIGARS (6059-8)
...PLETE BOOK OF PARROTS
...71-9)
...CARE MANUAL (5764-3)
...DFISH AND ORNAMENTAL
...RP (5634-5)
...E CARE MANUAL (5795-3)
...RINTH FISH (5635-3)

...NING GUIDE
...y illustrated with color photos,
... paperback.
...IUNICATING WITH YOUR DOG
...3-4)

...T AID FOR PETS
...ustrated, colorful guide, 20 pp.,
...ard with hanging chain and
... tabs.
...AID FOR YOUR CAT (5827-5)
...AID FOR YOUR DOG (5828-3)

ISBN prefix: 0-8120

Order from
your favorite
book or pet store

BARRON'S